# Windows 8.1

## GETTING STARTED GUIDE

 Saadat Wahid

Muzzammil Waheed

Ahmad Wahid

*Saadat Wahid, Muzzammil Waheed and Ahmad Wahid*

Right Protected Material

*Whole the written stuff, analyzed and presented in this book, such as tips and tricks along with other material is Right Protected Property. But, the name of Windows 8.1, the names of the functions of Windows 8.1, names of different windows referred in this book and all the functions about which the screenshots are displayed in this book are, specifically, the property of Microsoft, about which the Authors, Publishers, Sellers and Distributor don' have any concern.*

Disclaimer

*While every precaution has been taken in the preparation of this book, neither the authors, their sellers nor the distributors will be held liable for any damages, caused or alleged to be caused, either directly or indirectly, for errors and omissions, resulting from the use of information, contained in this book.*

ISBN-13: 978-1492796121
ISBN-10: 1492796123

# DEDICATION

*This Book is dedicated to All Prospects Users of Windows 8.1.*

*Saadat Wahid, Muzzammil Waheed and Ahmad Wahid*

# Table of Content at a Glance

# ACKNOWLEDGEMENT

*We, the Authors, acknowledge that it was not possible for us to write down this book without solid and really a constructive support from the experimental users of Windows 8 .*

*It was not possible without the solid feedback of the users of Windows 8.1 about the different functions, processes and applications of Windows 8.1*

*The help and cooperation of colleagues, friends, users of the Windows 8.1, some of the Microsoft partner developers and general observers without whose solid support, it was not possible for the authors to formulate the design and to accomplish the target of writing this book.*

*The efforts of all those who participated – directly or indirectly – in the development of this book are warmly appreciated and acknowledged.*

S.W.
M.W.
A.W.

*Saadat Wahid, Muzzammil Waheed and Ahmad Wahid*

**CHAPTER 1** >>>

# Selecting the Right Windows 8.1 Edition and Hardware

*Saadat Wahid, Muzzammil Waheed and Ahmad Wahid*

When you have decided to install and run the Windows 8.1, the updated version of Windows, 8 on your PC, the first thing you might want to consider is the edition which is best for you. Windows 8.1, like the Windows 8, has also been launched in many different editions which are designed, specifically, for specific users with differing interests.

# Windows 8.1 Editions

There are 4 different editions of Windows 8.1 but not all of them are appropriate for all users. Presently, following 4 editions are available for the general users:

> Home users can use Windows 8.1 Core edition.
> Professionals have the options to use Professional version.
> Windows 8.1 Enterprise edition is designed for the organizations, running a network of client computers. It is best for organizations who tend to install and manage the Windows 8.1 on all their server and client computers.

> **NOTE**
>
> Windows 8.1 Pro edition is installed by default when upgraded from Windows 8.

> The Windows RT 8.1 has been designed for low power consuming PC's running ARM architecture-based processors which are aimed at low pricing and longer battery.

# Selecting the Right and Most Suitable Version of Windows

Selecting the right Windows version is the first and foremost decision, a prospective users must take. Failing in reaching on right decision may cause you not to be able to utilize the Windows features up to satisfaction.

Similarly, if an expensive edition is purchased with a lot of features but not feasible to your optimum requirements, you may lose your precious resources.

Normal, consumers and developers are left with two editions of Windows 8.1 which can be installed, virtually, on any supported device disregarding whether it's an old desktop PC from your home, your work laptop or a tablet. These versions will be running, equally well, on all machines with a couple of different features.

## NOTE

Windows RT 8.1 can't run desktop (x86) apps like other Windows 8.1 versions.

# Comparison of All the 4 Versions of Windows 8.1

I have compiled the comparison of all the 4 versions of Windows 8.1, i.e. Windows RT 8.1, Windows 8.1 (Core Editions), Windows 8.1 (Pro Version) and Windows 8.1 (Enterprise Edition). This comparison has been produced in the Table 1, given below.

For the convenience of presentation, Table 1, shows the complete feature wise comparison of all the Windows 8.1 versions where, Windows 8.1 Pro has almost all the features other than those found in the Enterprise specific edition.

Windows Media Center is the only regular feature not found in the Core edition whereas, professional feature like remote desktop, VDI (virtual disk image) support, group policy and Hyper-V supports can only be found in Windows 8.1 Pro edition.

**Table 1:** Comparison of Features of 4 Different Versions of Windows 8.1 – Windows RT 8.1, Windows Core, Windows Pro and Windows Enterprise Editions.

Note: *For the Presentation Purpose, Availability of Specific Feature has been designated by Capital Word 'A' (Available) in Dark Blue while the Non Availability is Designated by 'NS (Not Supported)' in Red Color.*

| Features | RT 8.1 | Windows 8.1 Core | Pro | Enterprise |
|---|---|---|---|---|
| 3D printing support | A | A | A | A |
| AppLocker | NS | NS | NS | A |
| Apps launch other apps | A | A | A | A |
| Assigned access | A | NS | A | A |
| Automatic app updates from Windows Store | A | A | A | A |
| Binary extension scanning | A | A | A | A |
| Biometric enrollment | A | A | A | A |
| BitLocker and BitLocker To Go | NS | NS | A | A |
| BranchCache | NS | NS | NS | A |
| Built-in apps (Mail, Calendar, People, etc. | A | A | A | A |
| Built-in VPN clients | A | A | A | A |
| Client Hyper-V | NS | NS | A | A |
| CPU Sockets | 1 | 1 | 2 | 2 |
| Customize multiple tiles at once | A | A | A | A |
| Device Encryption | A | A | A | A |
| Device enrollment | A | A | A | A |
| DirectAccess | NS | NS | NS | A |
| Domain Join | NS | NS | A | A |
| Exchange ActiveSync | A | A | A | A |
| Family Safety | A | A | A | A |
| Four tile sizes | A | A | A | A |
| Group Policy | NS | Ns | A | A |
| Install and run desktop apps (86/64) | NS | A | A | A |
| InstantGo | A | A | A | A |
| Internet Explorer 11 | A | A | A | A |
| Lock screen photo slide show | A | A | A | A |
| Maximum RAM (**GB**) | 4 | 128 | 512 | 512 |
| Microsoft account login | A | A | A | A |
| Office Home & Student 2013 RT included | A | NS | NS | NS |
| MiraCast wireless display support | A | A | A | A |
| Mobile hotspot / Wi-Fi tethering | A | A | A | A |
| Mount ISO / VHDs | A | A | A | A |
| Multi-factor authentication for BYOD | A | A | A | A |
| Multiple instances of same app | A | A | A | A |

| | | | | |
|---|---|---|---|---|
| Multiple monitor improvements | A | A | A | A |
| Open MDM support | A | A | A | A |
| Open up to 4 variable sized windows at once | A | A | A | A |
| Optional boot to the desktop/All apps screen/Start screen | A | A | A | A |
| PC Settings improvements | A | A | A | A |
| Picture password | A | A | A | A |
| Portrait mode improvements | A | A | A | A |
| Precision touchpad improvements | A | A | A | A |
| Remote business data removal | A | A | A | A |
| Remote Desktop (client) | A | A | A | A |
| Remote Desktop (host) | A | A | A | A |
| Reset and refresh your PC | A | A | A | A |
| Search powered by Bing | A | A | A | A |
| Set desktop wallpaper as Start background | A | A | A | A |
| Sideloading LOB apps | NS | NS | NS | A |
| Start screen control | NS | NS | NS | A |
| Storage Spaces | NS | A | A | A |
| Switch languages on the fly (Language Packs) | A | A | A | A |
| The Start button | A | A | A | A |
| The Start screen and live tiles | A | A | A | A |
| Touch keyboard and thumb keyboard | A | A | A | A |
| Trusted Boot | A | A | A | A |
| VDI enhancements | NS | NS | NS | A |
| VHD boot | NS | NS | A | A |
| Wi-Fi Direct wireless printing support | A | A | A | A |
| Windows Defender | A | A | A | A |
| Windows Media Player | A | A | A | A |
| Windows SmartScreen | A | A | A | A |
| Windows Store | A | A | A | A |
| Windows To Go Creator | NS | NS | NS | A |
| Windows Update | A | A | A | A |
| Work folders | A | A | A | A |
| Workplace join | A | A | A | A |
| Xbox SmartGlass with Play To / Play On | A | A | A | A |
| | A | A | A | A |

# Which Edition is the Best for Whom?
## *For Home Users*

Home users may choose the Windows 8.1 (Core) edition, the cheapest one, yet providing all the needed features like:

➤ Entertainment
➤ Personalization
➤ Communication
➤ Customization
➤ And more

> **TIP**
>
> Media Center lovers, get the Windows 8.1 Pro Edition with Pro Pack.

As Windows 8.1 (Core) is also the edition which comes pre-installed on most of the devices, it is the recommended edition for home users who want to perform regular and common tasks.

People who are used to watching movies and recording TV shows might have to get the Pro edition since, the Media Center can only be installed in Windows 8.1 (Pro edition) after buying an upgrade key.

# Developers and Advanced Users

If you are a developer or advanced user, willing to use the advanced features of Windows 8.1, then you might want to get the Professional edition to get a hold of all advanced features. Windows 8.1 Professional edition offers mostly those features which are included in the update for Windows 8.

These features of Windows 8.1 are lucrative enough to appeal the users to get maximum benefits from this edition. Though the most costly one, but its purchase will open up the realm of Windows 8.1 features and api's for you.

# Other Editions and Their Usages
## *Windows RT*

Windows RT can't be found in retail in DVDs or ISOs since, it comes pre-installed in Windows RT based devices. Older Windows RT devices running Windows 8 would, automatically, be updated to Windows RT 8.1 from Store. But, you won't have the choice to install any other edition of Windows 8.1 on your Windows RT based device due to restrictions, imposed by Microsoft.

# Windows 8.1 Enterprise

Enterprises and businesses can use Windows 8.1 Enterprise Edition for their PC's which would let them get the advanced enterprise specific features like bio-metric unlock, Start Screen restriction, Windows To GO, apps installation restrictions and many other security and advanced features.

# Hardware Requirements

Windows 8.1, being an update for Windows 8, runs perfectly on any device which can run Windows 8 and Windows 7. Windows 8.1 has got some ease in requirements which makes running Windows 8.1 on your old PC's easier.

Any compatible device with a couple of years old hardware can run Windows 8.1, easily, without any glitches. To help you consider whether your PC can run Windows 8.1 or not, Microsoft has suggested the minimum hardware requirements to run it.

# Primary Hardware Requirements

For the details, see the Table 2:

**Table 2:** Hardware Requirements for Windows 8.1 (Recommended)

| Hardware | Requirements |
| --- | --- |
| Processor | 1 gigahertz (GHz) or faster |
| RAM | 1 gigabyte (GB) for 32-bit (x86) or 2 GB for 64-bit (x64) |
| Free hard disk space | 16 GB while installing 32-bit (x86) version or 20 GB for 64-bit (x64) |
| | Windows RT 8.1 requires at least 12GB of free storage to upgrade |
| Graphics card | Microsoft DirectX 9 graphics device with WDDM driver |

**Optional requirements**

- ➢ 64-bit version installation requires CMPXCHG16b, PrefetchW and LAHF/SAHF support for your processor
- ➢ A touch screen to use the touch features of Windows 8.1
- ➢ Minimum of 1024 x 768 pixels of screen resolution to run Modern-UI apps including Store
- ➢ An active Internet connection to access Store

*Saadat Wahid, Muzzammil Waheed and Ahmad Wahid*

**CHAPTER 2** ▶▶▶

# Personalization

*Saadat Wahid, Muzzammil Waheed and Ahmad Wahid*

Let's start this chapter with Start Screen, which is also known as the Modern User Interface also known as Modern UI.

Start Screen, first introduced in Windows 8, has been modified, pretty much, in Windows 8.1. The following changes have been made in the Start Screen:

1. The First Change in Start Screen of Windows 8.1, as you will note, is the introduction of four different sizes of tiles. The tiniest one is 1 x 1 while the huge one is 4 x 4 along with two from Windows 8, i.e. 2 x 2 and 2 x 3.

2. In Windows 8.1, some changes have been made to customize method as compared to Windows 8.

# Enabling Customization of Start Screen

If you want to customize your Start Screen, what you will have to do is to:

1. Right Click anywhere on the Start Screen or swipe from bottom. A Customize, similar to the one displayed in Figure 1, will popup.
2. Here, press 'Customize' button.

Press Here to Start Customization of Your Windows

Figure 1: Customization of Start Screen

3. Now, your customization has been enabled.

# Resizing Tiles

If you want to customize the tile size of one or more apps, follow the instruction:

1. Simply enable the Customization.
2. Select the tiles you want to resize
3. Once selected, press the Resize button in the bottom app bar.

> **TIP**
>
> You can also resize the desktop app tiles on Start Screen but, you will only get two different sizes to select from.

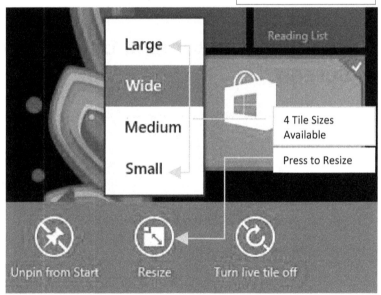

Figure 2: Resizing the Tiles

4. Here, you will get four different options for tile sizes, such as:

   ➢ Small
   ➢ Medium
   ➢ Wide
   ➢ Large

5. Now, select your desired size.

6. Selected apps would be resized according to the selected option and their current size.

# Moving Tiles

One new option, available in the Windows 8.1, is the multiple tiles move option, i.e. you can now move two or more apps at a time as a group.

Simply, follow the instructions:

## NOTE

If you have multiple tiles selected, selecting to resize would affect all of them and they would be resized depending on the current situation.

➢ Simply press the apps by right clicking or tapping.

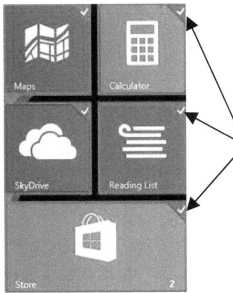

Indication that a Tile has been selected and can be customized

Figure 3: Moving Tiles

➢ Hold it on.
➢ Move the apps by dragging them to the desired positions. That's all!

## TIP

You will notice a group of apps as one tile while moving but, don't worry, you would get the order of those apps back once you leave the apps at the destination.

# Live Tiles Option

Windows 8.1, just like the Windows 8, displays the Live Tiles of apps. Here the information from within apps is displayed on the tiles of the apps even when the apps are not operational. The apps are updated, frequently in background to provide up to date information.

Figure 4: A Live Tile Example

The Live Tile feature is every helpful in most of the features since you can see what's the latest information from that app. But, sometimes the app(s) start showing confidential information so, you might want to disable it/them.

Follow the steps below to disable live tiles of app(s):

➢ Right click or tap and hold to enable customization for that app.
➢ You would get the 'Turn live tile off' option in the app bar. Pressing it would disable live tiles (See Figure 5).

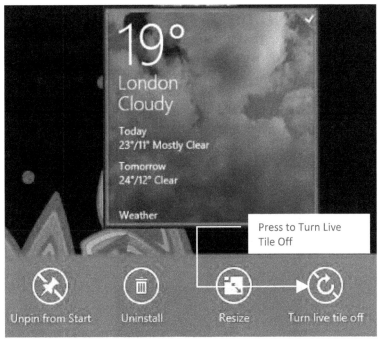

Figure 5: Moving Tiles Option

# App Groups

Windows 8.1, just like Windows 8, lets you create app groups and name them to your desired ones. App Grouping and their naming have been made very easy with Windows 8.1.

Simply enable the customization and move your apps to separate location where multiple apps would make a group.

You can create a new group by moving the apps between two groups where a white vertical line will display the place where a new group would be created.

# Sorting

You can make different groups of apps on your Start Screen with your desired apps in each.

# Group Name

Simply enable the Customization option by swiping from bottom or right clicking and selecting the 'Customize'.

Once your customization option is enabled, you would see the name group option on top of each app group.

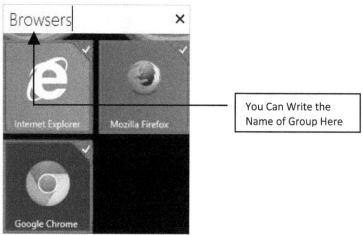

Figure 6: Naming the Group

Here, you can type whatever name you like to give to your group.

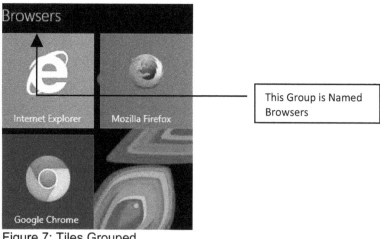

Figure 7: Tiles Grouped

# Pin/Unpin

Windows 8.1 also includes the option to pin or unpin from Start Screen or you can pin tiles from 'All app' section to Start Screen.

## *Pin*

If you want to pin a tile from 'All apps' section to Start Screen of Windows 8, simply go to the 'All apps' by pressing the down arrow on left side of Start Screen or by swiping from down.

➤ You would be taken to the 'All apps' section. Here search for your desired app which you want to be pinned to Start Screen.

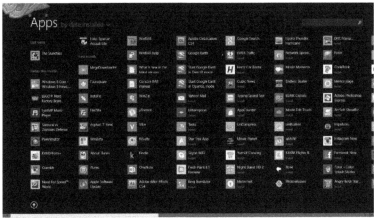

Figure 8: All Apps Section

➤ Select the app tile by pressing and holding it or by right clicking on it. Once selected, you can press 'Pin to Start' button to pin the tile to Start Screen which would appear at the end of the Start Screen.

# Unpin

You can unpin apps from Start Screen easily just like Windows 8.

Simply tap and hold down or right click on the app tile you want to unpin from Start Screen and press 'Unpin from start' from app bar.

## TIP

You can also select multiple apps from 'All apps' section and then pin them to Start Screen at once.

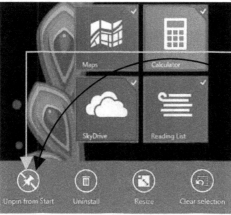

Press to Unpin

Figure 9: Unpinning from Start Screen

# Uninstall

Windows 8.1 lets you uninstall apps easily in few steps but, the steps for desktop and Modern-UI apps are different.

# Modern-UI Apps

First select the app(s) you want to uninstall by tap and holding gesture or by right click on its tile. Once selected, press the Uninstall button from bottom app bar.

## TIP

You can also unpin multiple app tiles at once by selecting multiple tiles by tap and holding or right clicking and then, selecting 'Unpin from start'.

22

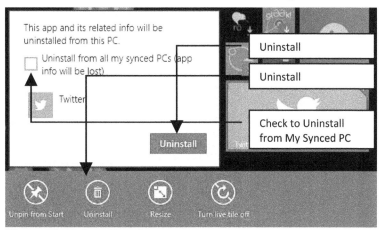

Figure 10: Uninstalling Apps

> ➢ A pop-up menu would appear, asking 'This/These app/apps and its/their related info will be deleted from all your synced PC's'.

> ➢ Desktop: If, you are uninstalling a desktop (x86) app then, the steps are a bit long.

> ➢ First select the app tile you want to 'Uninstall' by tap and holding or by right click either from Start Screen or from 'All apps' section.

>   You would be shown the app bar on bottom.

> ➢ Press 'Uninstall'.

> ➢ You would be taken to desktop where 'Program and Features' window will open.

> ➢ You would be taken to desktop where 'Program and Features' window will open.

Figure 11: Programs and Features

➢ Here you can select the apps to uninstall which would take you through the whole step-by-step uninstallation process as was done in Windows 7.

# All Apps

The 'All apps' screen of Windows 8.1 where all the installed desktop and Modern-UI apps can be found has changed a lot. You just don't find the apps there but, you can sort them in different ways.

All Apps section is where you will find the latest installed apps from Store and desktop whereas, the Start Screen won't get the app tiles pinned just like Windows 8.

## TIP

It is important that you select appropriate option whether to remove the app(s) only from this PC or from all of your synced (connected) PC's.

If, you want to remove the app(s) only from this PC then, check the option named 'Only from this PC' otherwise, simply press the Uninstall button to remove apps from all your PCs.

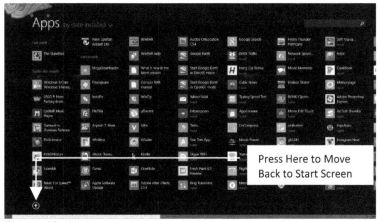

Figure 12: All Apps

➢ Once you want to go to the All apps screen of Windows 8.1,
swipe down on your touch screen device or press the down
arrow button on the bottom left corner of Start Screen.

Your 'All apps' section will open up.

# Sorting Apps

The All apps section of Windows 8.1 lets you sort the app listing
in different styles. Simply press by 'Date Installed' button
alongside the 'Apps' heading.

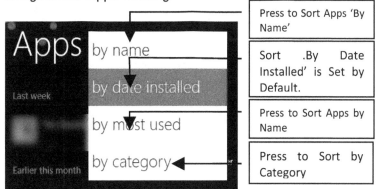

Figure 13: Sorting of Apps

You can select from different options like date installed, name, most used and category etc. which would sort the apps in that manner.

# Semantic Zoom

You can also use the Semantic zoom option to view the overview of all your installed desktop and apps.

Semantic Zoom also works in different ways like date of installed, will show the dates, 'most used' will show the frequency of apps used, name would show a list of alphabets from which the app names starts and category will show the app categories.

Figure 14: Semantic Zoom on All Apps Section

Sematic Zoom can be accessed by pressing the '-' sign on bottom right corner or pinching if you are using a touch screen device.

Semantic Zoom feature of Windows 8.1 lets you see all your Start Screen apps at once and if you have a lot of app tiles pinned to your Start Screen then, it can help you get to your desired apps easily.

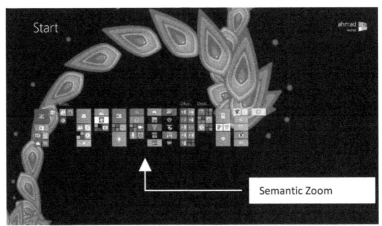

Figure 15: Semantic Zoom on Start Screen

Simply press the '-' button on bottom right corner of Start Screen of pinch to zoom out and use sematic zoom feature.

*Saadat Wahid, Muzzammil Waheed and Ahmad Wahid*

**CHAPTER 3** »»

# Hidden Features

*Saadat Wahid, Muzzammil Waheed and Ahmad Wahid*

The fifth and probably the most important Charm of the Charms Bar of Windows 8.1 is the Settings.

It holds the options of whole OS and everything from customizations to privacy whereas sharing settings can also be accessed from this Charm.

This is a display of your PC on bottom of Settings Charm where your network status, Volume Control, Screen Settings, Keyboard Settings, Notification and Power options can be seen.

If you press the Settings from the Desktop, the appearing window will be the Figure given below:

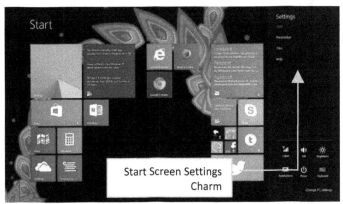

Figure 16: Start Settings Charm

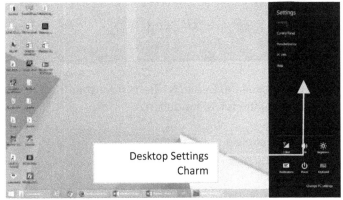

Figure 17: Desktop Settings Charm

31

# Start Screen and Desktop Charms Bar

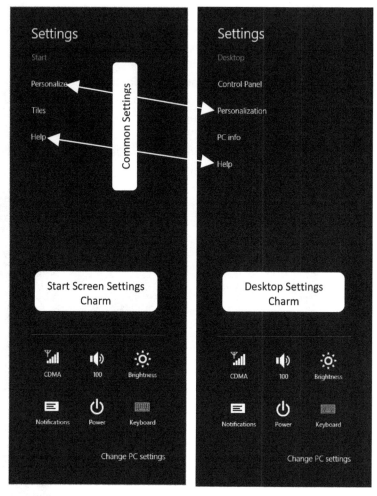

If you access the Settings Charm from your Start Screen then you would get the following options:

1. Personalize
2. Tiles
3. Help

# Personalize

Personalize holds the personalization options like the colors and accent settings of Modern-UI of Windows 8.1 as well as the Start Screen background options.

## NOTE

You can also set the desktop wallpaper as the Start Screen background.

Figure 18: Setting

Press Personalize for the Personalization

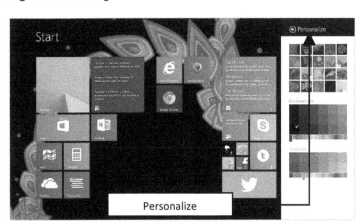

Figure 19: Personalize

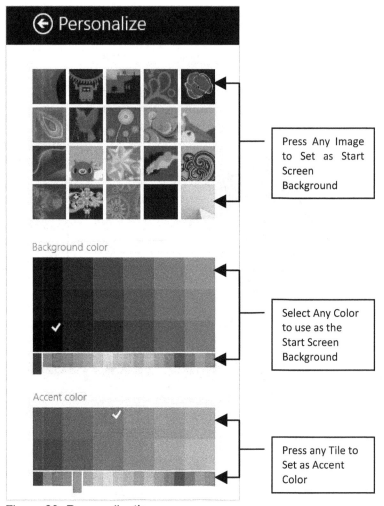

Figure 20: Personalization

# Tiles

Tiles option in the Settings Charm of Windows 8.1 on Start Screen lets you select whether to show the Administrative tiles on the Start Screen or not.

1. Just press the Personalize.
2. Pressing the Personalize will open up the Tile Setting popup.

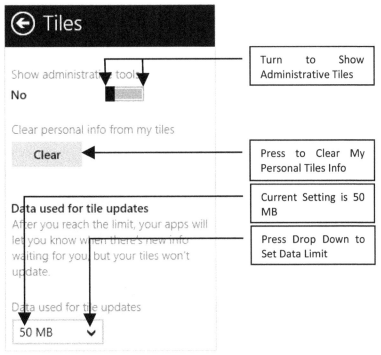

Figure 21: Tiles Charm

# Administrative Tiles

Administrative Tools hold the tiles from advanced section of Control Panel which is accessed, normally, by professionals.

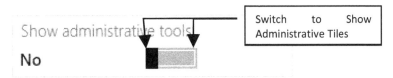

Figure 22: Showing Administrative Tiles

# Tile Updates

Another option in the Tiles section is the tile updates. The Start Screen displays live tiles of apps where live information from apps is displayed but, if you ever want to clear the live tiles information then, you can press 'Clear' under 'clear personal information from tiles'.

# Clearing Personal Info from Tiles

If you want to clear personal info about the Tiles from your memory of computer, press the Clear Button.

Figure 23: Clearing Personal Info

# Data Used for Tiles Updates

One more useful thing under Tiles section is the ability to control how much data is consumed by your live tiles. You can select from a number of options and unlimited data can also be used and if limit is specified, the tiles will stop updating live.

**NOTE**

Set this limit if you are using a metered connection where you have to pay for extra data.

If you are using a unlimited connection and always want to get latest information from apps as live tiles then, you may select unlimited.

With 50 MB default, you may select data used for tile updates to Unlimited.

Figure 24: Data for the Tile Updates Set

Upon pressing this drop down, a menu displaying 6 following data limits will open up to provide you option to select one for your PC:

1. 50 MB
2. 100 Mb
3. 200 MB
4. 300 MB
5. 400 MB
6. Unlimited

# Help
# Start Screen Charms Help

Upon pressing Help at the Tiles Charm of Start Screen, the Help link will open up a browser where the FAQs about Windows 8.1 would be displayed from official Microsoft.com site[1] - see Foot Note for URL.

---

[1] http://windows.microsoft.com/en-US/windows-8/start-screen-faq

Figure 25: Start Screen FAQ

# Desktop Tiles Help

On the other hand, pressing the Desktop Tiles Help will open up different window.

## NOTE

The Help articles in the Windows Help and Support page need an active internet connection to work.

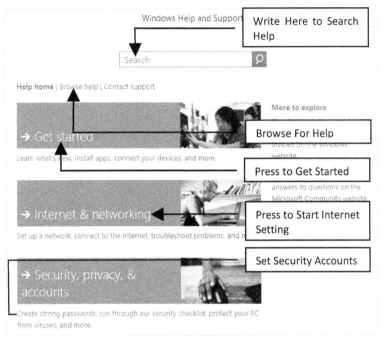

Figure 26: Windows Help and Support

The official web site of the Microsoft website for the Windows help can be seen in Figure above.

The Help link in the Windows 8.1 Settings Charm will take you to the Windows Help and Support page where all the help related to Windows 8.1 and its features can be found.

# App Settings

The Settings Charms of Windows 8.1 also holds the options of apps when accessed while the app is open. Here, you can get different options related to app like options, graphics, audio, controls etc.

**NOTE**

App Settings may differ from app to app.

For the illustration purposes, I have selected the Mail app, one of the most common app in Windows 8.1. When I opened its Settings, following options appeared:

Figure 27: Mail App Settings

1. Accounts
2. Options
3. Help
4. About
5. Feedback
6. Permissions
7. Rate & Review

Here, I will discuss only those settings which are common in each app, such as, Permissions, About and Options.

# Permissions

The permission page in the Settings Charm is app specific and appears while using an app.

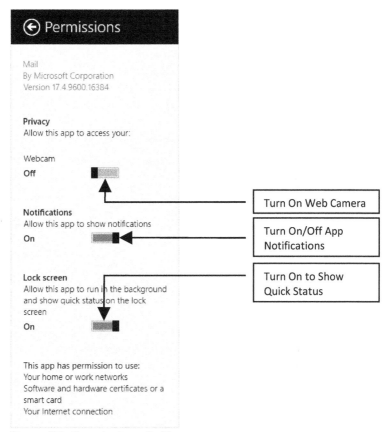

Figure 28: Permissions Settings

The Permissions tab shows you the permissions which the app has.

You can also turn On / Off different app permissions like camera access, location access and more.

**NOTE**

Default Status of Switches:

WebCam      Off
Notification   On
Lock Screen   On

# About

The about page in Settings Charm shows the app's about page and it only appears in apps and are app specific.

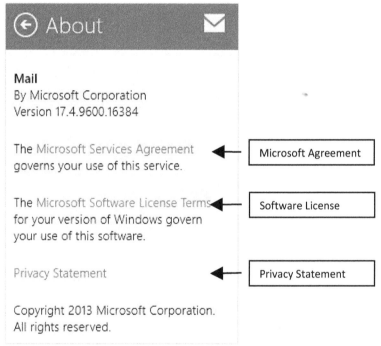

Figure 29: About Setting

You can read about the app's descriptions, its version number and the developer details in this page.

# Options

The Options page in Settings Charm holds the options which are specific to each and every apps. The options like controls, behavior etc. can be found in this page.

# Desktop

If you access the Settings Charm from anywhere on the desktop then, you would come across the settings like Control Panel, personalization, PC info and Help.

# Control Panel

Pressing the Control Panel link in the Desktop Tiles Settings will open up the classic Windows 7 style Control Panel on desktop where different options can be accessed.

Figure 30: Traditional Windows 7 and Windows 8 Style Contro Panel

As the Control Panel has nothing new and is as per Windows 7, I it would not be discussed further.

# PC Info

The PC Info link in the Settings Charm takes you to the System information page of Control Panel from desktop where all the details of your PC and Windows, Windows version, Windows architecture and your hardware specifications, can be seen.

You will also get the status of your Windows 8.1 PC there; whether it is activated or now. You can also change the product key of your Windows 8 from there.

When you will click open the PC info, following information will be available to you about your PC:

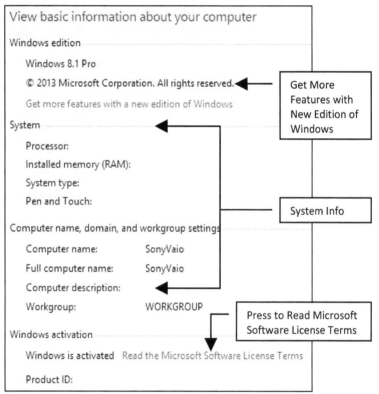

Figure 31: PC Info

# Edition

> System
> Processor
> System Type
> Pen and Touch

1. Computer Name: (full computer name), Computer description, domain and workgroup settings.
2. Windows Activation
3. Product ID

In the side bar, you will be offered following option settings:

1. Device Manager
2. Remote settings
3. System protection
4. Advanced system settings
5. Action Center
6. Windows Update

To change the status / Setting or Activate Windows, press here.

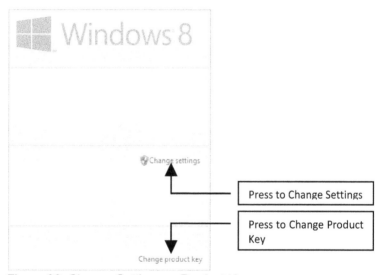

Figure 32: Change Settings or Product Key

# PC Status and Control Icons

The Settings Charm of Windows 8.1, just like Windows 8, also shows PC Status and the Control icons which remain there throughout the OS whether it's an app, Start Screen or desktop.

These icons are the basic control of your Windows and can be accessed, easily, from anywhere.

Figure 33: PC Status & Control Icons

The icons include four different things:

# Network Connection

The first icon on left of Settings Charm is the network connectivity icon where you can check the network status of your PC. You will get different info there like:

➢ Whether your PC is connected to a Wi-Fi connection or not.
➢ If connected, the name of Wi-Fi connection would be showed.
➢ Broadband connection will also be showed with connection type.
➢ Other connections will be showed with the Ethernet connection icon.

You also get 'Not connected' icon if you aren't connected to any network.

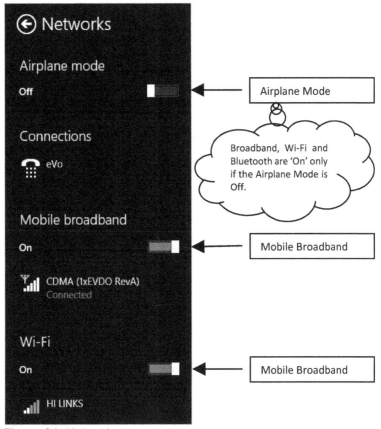

Figure 34: Networks

Pressing any network connection icon takes you to the Network status in Charm Bar where all the network connection are showed and their details can also be seen.

# Volume

The second icon on the Settings Charm is the Volume Control icon which lets you control the volume of your PC.

**NOTE**

Default Status

Airplane Mode    Off
Mobile Broadband
On
Wi-Fi              On

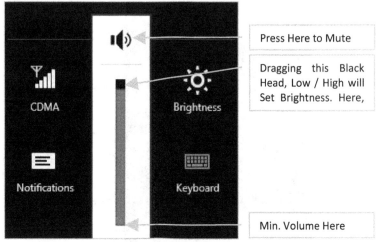

Figure 35: Volume Control Icon

It just shows a slider which can be moved up or down to adjust volume.

# Brightness / Screen Options

The third option is the screen option where you can adjust the brightness of your screen and also turn on/off the orientation of your screen if it's a tablet or mobile device.

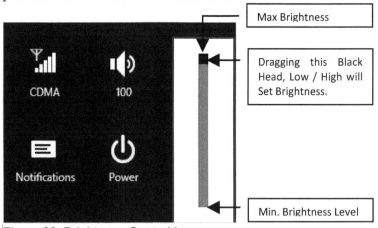

Figure 36: Brightness Control Icon

# Notifications

The notifications icon on the Settings Charm lets you select the notification delay timings of notifications.

You can select from three different options of delay i.e. 1, 3 and 8 hours.

## NOTE

If the notifications are disabled from PC Settings then, you would be able to set notification delay timing but, notification won't be enabled.

# Power

The fifth option is the Power which holds the power options of your PC.

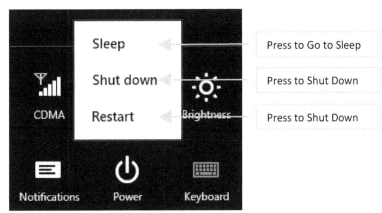

Figure 37: Power Control Icon

You can choose to shutdown, restart, hibernate or sleep your PC from there.

# Keyboard

The last option in the Settings Charm is the keyboard options where you can select the overall layouts of your keyboard, configure touch screen keyboard of Windows 8 and see how it appears.

*Saadat Wahid, Muzzammil Waheed and Ahmad Wahid*

**CHAPTER 4** ▶▶

# Charms Bar

After going through personalization of newly-installed Windows 8.1, let's start working on Charms Bar (Settings).

The Charms Bar is the one step options menu for all the necessary settings, options and features of Windows 8.1.

Microsoft has also made the Charms Bar the 'one step option' to search the whole OS, share files and other things, access devices and go to Settings of apps and OS easily.

# Accessing the Charms Bar

Charms Bar can be accessed by adopting one of the two methods:

1.You may swipe from right side of screen anywhere in Windows 8.1 to the top from bottom.

2.Alternatively, you may move your mouse cursor to top from bottom right corner and/or from top to bottom on right corner.

Figure 38: Charms Bar

# Options Available in the Charms Bar

As seen in the above Figure, Windows 8.1 includes a total of five following options in the Charms Bar (Settings):

1. Search
2. Share
3. Start
4. Devices
5. Settings.

Let's have a closer look upon each of them, one by one

# Search Charm

The Search Charm is the search engine of all your apps in OS and you can type anything in the Search Charms disregarding where you are in OS. From here, Windows can search everything on your PC and the internet and show the most appropriate results.

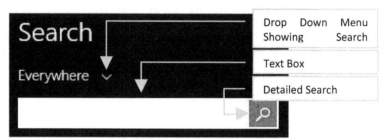

Figure 39: Search

When you will tap on Search at the Charms Bar, the following window will display a textbox and a drop down menu in the top right corner, as displayed in the above Figure.

When you Drop Down is tapped, the drop down will display a menu offering five different options / Filters for the users to select from and apply with each having different usage.

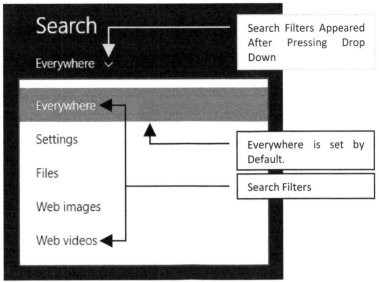

Figure 40: Search Filters

# Search Filters

You can also select from five different filters for search results on Start Screen by selecting them from top of search bar.

# Everywhere

By default, Everywhere is selected which will search for everything on your PC and internet. It displays appropriate results from every category including:

**NOTE**

Everywhere is Set on 'On' by Default.

1.  Files
2.  Web results
3.  Videos and more.

Pressing any result will open the Search app where detailed results are showed.

# Settings

The Settings filter in Search will let you search only for settings. Selecting Settings as filter will only show the results from your PC which includes the Settings only.

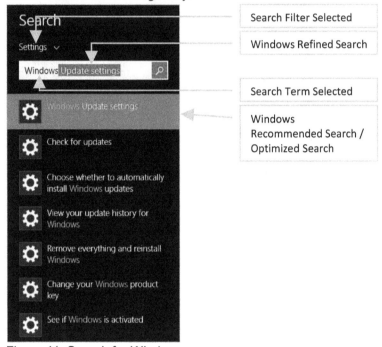

Figure 41: Search for Windows

# Files

The files filter, just like Settings, will show you the files from your PC. You would be showed all the files from your PC, related to your searched keyword.

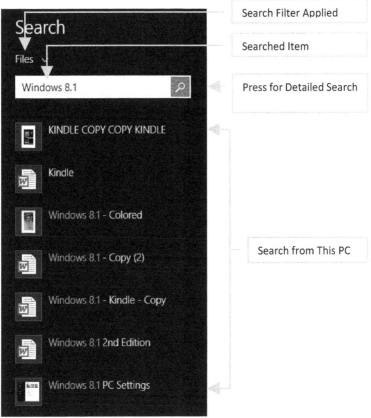

Figure 42: Applying File Filter

# Web Images

If you prefer to search images on web and don't want to visit the web browser then, Windows 8.1 has got you covered. Just type anything in the Search Charm of Windows 8.1 and select the 'Web images'.

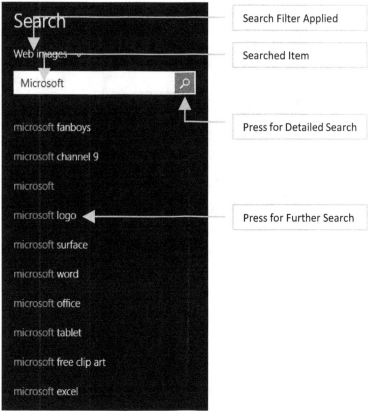

Figure 43: Applying the Web Search Filter

Related results would be displayed below the search bar which, on tapping, will take you to Search app where the images related to your searched keyword would be displayed.

# Web Images – Sizing Filters

You can also apply different filters to the image results by selecting them from bottom app bar. Filters like size, colors, type, layout and people can be applied which will filter the images according to the selected item.

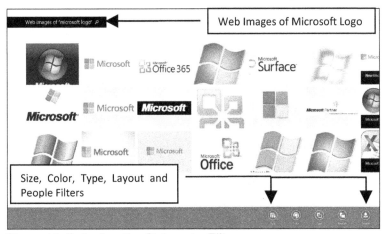

Figure 44: Selecting the Sizing etc. Filters

Following filters can be seen here in this app:

1. Size
2. Color
3. Type
4. Layout
5. People

Size, Color, Type, Layout & People Filters

Figure 45: Five Sizing etc. Filters

# Web Videos

Typing anything in the Search Charm and selecting 'Web videos' filter from filters will open the video results in the Search app. The video results will include videos from every source like YouTube, Vimeo, Daily Motion and others.

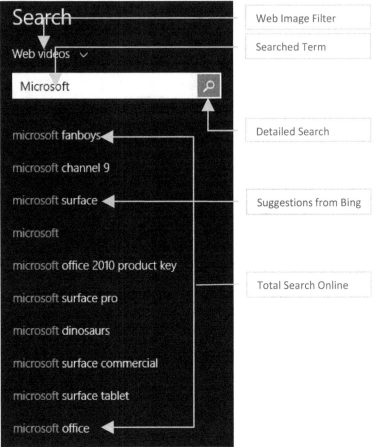

Web Image Filter

Searched Term

Detailed Search

Suggestions from Bing

Total Search Online

Figure 46: Web Videos Search Filter

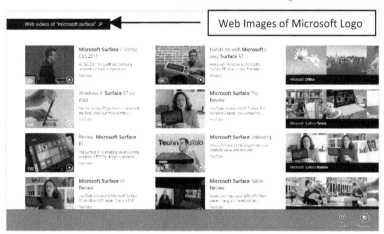

Figure 47: Web Videos of Microsoft Surface

# Web Videos – Length & Resolution Filters

You can also apply different filters to the video results in the search app of Windows 8.1. Filters like Duration and Resolution can be accessed by opening up the app by swiping from bottom or right pressing / clicking.

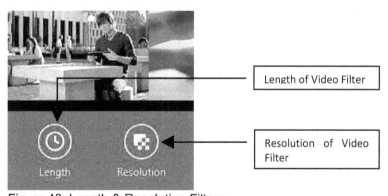

Figure 48: Length & Resolution Filters

# Detailed Search

The best and most awesome feature of Windows 8.1 is the Search app which shows results from everything including the following:

1.  Music
2.  Videos
3.  Images
4.  Web pages
5.  Results from Windows Store.

The detailed and rich search results can be obtained by selecting 'Everywhere' filter from Search Charm.

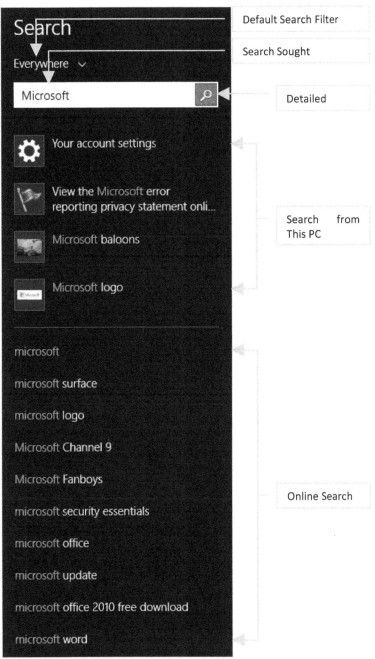

Figure 49: Everywhere Search Filter

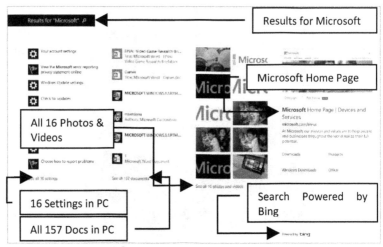

Figure 50: Detailed Search

# Settings

The first thing in the Search app of Windows 8.1, available in the Settings of your PC, can be selected to access different settings. You can press the 'See all [number]' link to see all results related to Settings.

It is noticeable that if you are searching for something which isn't really a setting in your PC then, the Settings result might not appear.

# My Documents

The second thing after the Settings in the Search app will be the Documents from your PC. All the documents in your PC with the name related to your searched keyword will appear. Selecting any will open the document in the appropriate app.

# My Photos & Videos

The third thing on the search results would be the My Photos & My Videos where all the photos from your PC would be displayed along with the videos from your hard drive.

# Web Results

If you searched for something and nothing is found in your PC then related to your search, the search app also includes the option to show the web results.

The web results, powered by Microsoft Bing, shows the most appropriate results on start followed by least relevant results to the right.

When you think you have found the result of your query, simply press the web page link and the website would open in your default browser.

# Windows Store Results

Windows 8.1 not just displays the results from your PC and from the web but you will also be shown the most relevant apps to your query and the links to the Store of apps are showed just after the web results.

Pressing any app would open the Store app of Windows 8.1 in snap mode where the download and detail-page of the app would be showed.

# Images and Videos

If, you think you couldn't find the appropriate thing in the search either from your PC or from the web pages then, you might select the Images or Videos filters from the end of the app where Images or Video results would be shown only.

# Related Searches

If you don't choose the images or videos filter from the end of the search app, you would start seeing the related search results from Bing which keeps on appearing and doesn't have any end.

# Rich results

If you search for everything from the Search Charm on Start Screen and your searched keyword includes the name of some celebrity, artist or some other popular person then, you would be shown completely different results in the search app.

For instance, if you search for a music artist, you would be shown his/her name first where his/her birth date would be shown beside the picture and the genre, country and other information is showed beside that.

You can also choose to play songs from that artist right from the page or you can read the complete biography of the artist using the Wikipedia app which is an optional install to view biography. You are also shown the most recent songs of that artist in column which is highlighted in different color to make it more catchy.

The albums, videos and the images of the artist are also shown followed by the regular web results, followed by apps and image/video filters.

# Share Charm

The second item in the Charms Bar of Windows 8.1 is the Share Charm, used mainly for sharing purposes. Share Charm is useful in every function where you want to share something from Windows 8.1 to web, an app or on the internet.

When you will press the Share, the resulting window is displayed below:

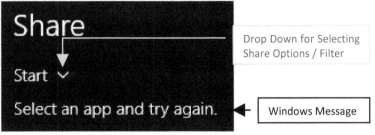

Figure 51: Share Charm

When you will press the Share Drop Down menu, the resulting menu is displayed below:

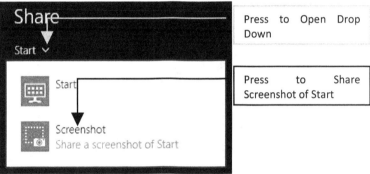

Figure 52: Sharing a Screenshot of Start

Share Charm of Windows 8 had, no doubt, very useful options where you could share different things from apps, OS and/or web to other apps.

But, with Windows 8.1, the Share Charm's functions have been enhanced to get more sharing features and you can even share the screenshot of the screen directly to other apps.

# Screenshot

Although Windows 8.1, just like Windows 8, lets you take screenshot of your screen by pressing the 'Windows Key + Print screen' keys but, with Windows 8.1, you also get a feature of screenshot sharing where the Windows takes the screen of your screen, automatically, and lets you share the screen, directly, to apps like People, Mail and/or SkyDrive where the images are uploaded to the folder of your choice.

Simply swipe from right and select Share or press the 'Windows key + H' to open the Share Charm.

Depending upon the options of the app, you would get the Sharing options. Here you select the screenshot option from the drop down menu just below the 'Share' text.

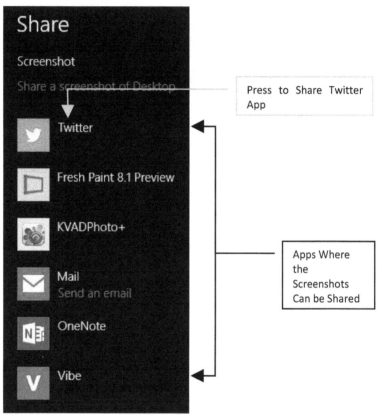

Figure 53: Sharing a Screenshot

Once 'screenshot' is selected, you would be asked to select the app, you want to share the screenshot.

Once you have selected the app to share, your Share Charm will close and your screen will flash for a second. Now, the selected app will open in the Share charm where you can share the screenshot.

Figure 54: App Sharing

# Reading List

One of the best addition in the Share Charm of Windows 8.1 is the inclusions of Reading List app. Reading List app is a bookmarking app of Windows 8.1 where you can save all your bookmarks for future reference.

Reading List is fully compatible with the Share Charm of Windows 8.1 and you can add anything to the app using the Share Charm.

**NOTE**

As Reading List app can bookmark the webpages, so if you are trying to save something else then, you would be disappointed.

Whenever, you think you need to save some webpage, simply swipe from right and select the Share Charm or press the 'Windows key + H' button which will open the Share Charm.

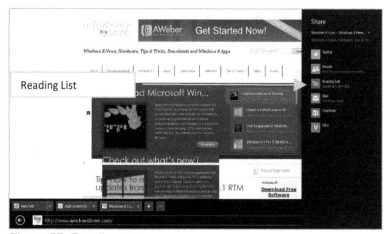

Figure 55: Reading List

Once opened, a list of supported apps will be displayed to which you can share. Reading List would be among them if you are trying to save the URL of a webpage.

Once the Reading List is selected, the Share Charm will open the Reading List app. Here you would be showed what is being saved by Windows.

Figure 56: How to Add to Reading List

# Devices

The Devices Charm of Windows 8.1 holds the options like the device connectivity and playing to different device options.

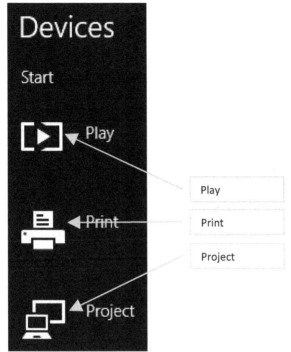

Figure 57: Window Displaying Devices

Pressing the Devices will open the window displaying the Devices. Let's have a closer look upon each of these.

# Play

The Play option in the 'Devices' is the remote control of your PC which lets you connect and play different functions to other connected devices like Windows 8/8.1 powered devices, your Xbox controller, HD TV and many more supported devices.

**NOTE**

Upon pressing the Play, you will see the message; 'You can only Play from Apps'.

The Play feature works mostly from audio and video apps like Xbox Music and Xbox Videos app where you can play the music or video to your Xbox, other PC and/or HD TV using the Wi-Fi and Microsoft account.

Some of the games for Windows 8/8.1 also support the 'Play to' feature which can be used to switch the game playing to your HD TV, Xbox console or any other device.

Figure 58: Message to Play Music with Apps

# Print

The Print option is the one press-support to print documents using your connected printer. Simply press the Print button from Devices Charm and you would get the option to print the selected docs, images etc. from screen using your printer, connected to your machine.

**NOTE**

You must be using a supported printer with your Windows 8.1 PC in-order to take advantage of the Print option in Devices Charm.

You would need to select something from an app on screen like a text, a webpage or an image etc. which can be printed using your Printer.

Figure 59: Message to Print with App

# Project

Upon pressing the Project, you will see the window: see next Figure.

Although, the project option differs from device to device like second monitor will show some other options while a projector or multimedia will show different options. In the project, you would be offered four different options:

# PC Screen

Being the default, using this option you can use on the default screen of your PC to show things. Other screens would remain un-projected.

# Multi-Monitor

If you have connected a second monitor to your PC and want to project screen to it, you simply have to select the Project option.

**BONUS**

Don't forget to take advantage of the snap mode in extend option of screen where you can use more than one apps at once.

Figure 60: Project Window

# Duplicate Screen

This option is best if you want to show the same screen on external device, such as multimedia, as you see on your default one. After selecting this option, you will be able to see your screen on external devices. You can customize the settings about second duplicate screen by going to PC Settings.

# Extend

Extend option gives you the capabilities to extend your screen to more than one. This option will give you the capability to use different apps on different screens which would help you multi-task easily.

You can use both desktop and modern-UI apps on different screens.

# Second Screen

If you are connecting your PC to a HD TV or any other device and only want that screen to work, this option is best for you. Using this option, you can turn-off the default screen of your device and the second screen will keep working.

You can customize the settings about second screen only by going to PC Settings.

**CHAPTER 5**

# PC and Devices

Chapter on PC Settings describes the new features added recently in the Windows 8.1.

Windows 8.1 has got a whole new PC Settings app where all the important options from Control Panel of desktop have been moved. This PC Settings is fully 'touch friendly' and makes the configuration of your PC more fun.

All the settings in the PC Settings of Windows 8.1 have been categorized according to categories and sub-categories to help you find your desired settings easily.

# Change PC Settings

To open the PC Setting, you need to do one of the following things:

1. Either search for PC Settings using Search Charm of Windows 8.1.
2. Alternatively, press the Change PC Settings link in the Settings Charm (*Windows Key + I*).

Here, you will see the two major parts / columns of the page with various options, available in both the columns:

1.  Left Column: PC Setting
2.  Right Colum: Top Setting

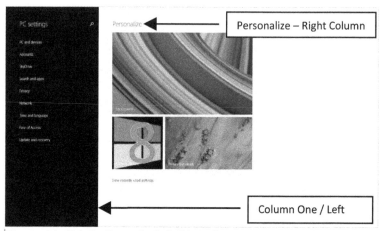

Figure 61: PC Setting - Left & Right Columns

# Left Column (*PC Settings*)

1. PC & Devices
2. Accounts
3. SkyDrive
4. Search & App
5. Privacy
6. Network
7. Time and Language
8. Ease of Access
9. Update and Recovery

Figure 62: Left Column / Column One- PC Setting

# Column Two / Right Column (Top Settings)

1. Lock Screen
2. Account Picture
3. Picture Password
4. Slide Show
5. Lock Screen Apps
6. Password
7. Pin
8. Hear What's on the Screen

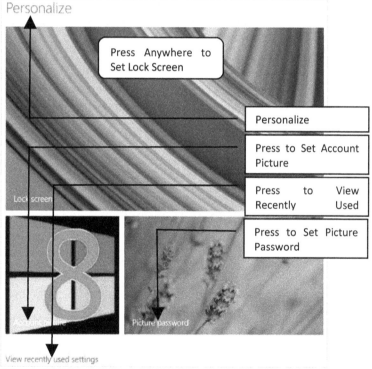

Figure 63: Personalize

Now, we will discuss each of the settings, available in the PC Settings.

The PC Settings app by default shows all the top and most important settings under the 'Top Settings' tab where the most important and the frequently access settings of PC Settings are showed.

The things which remain there each and every time are the lock screen, account picture and the picture passwords whose thumbnails remain on top of page.

Pressing any settings under Top Settings page will take you to its dedicated page where complete settings can be found.

# Left Column – PC & Devices (*Lock Screen*)

The Lock Screen tab of PC Settings holds the options related to the lock screen of your Windows.

Here you can select the lock screen image, control the notifications shown on it and see how the image is shown on lock screen and other settings.

# Lock Screen Image

The Lock Screen image selection page, entitled as the 'Preview', lets you select the lock screen image of your PC for your own account.

In Lock Screen Preview, you are offered to select from the most recent lock screen images or press the 'Browse' button to select your own desired image.

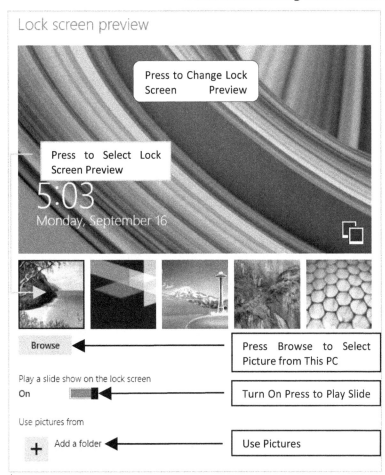

Figure 64: Lock Screen Preview

Upon pressing the Browse button, the emerging screen will be like this (depending upon your PC settings):

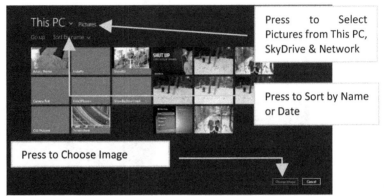

Figure 65: Selection of Images from This PC, Sorting or Go Up

# Selection from This PC

You can select the lock screen image from a number of locations like:

1. Your PC
2. Libraries
3. SkyDrive
4. Network Location
5. From an app

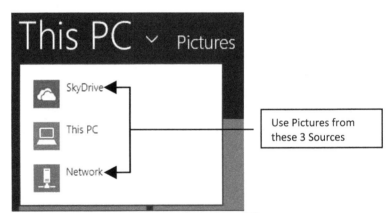

Figure 66: Selection of Image from This PC

# Slide Show

You can also set up a slideshow as the lock screen image where different images, selected by you, are shown in random order, size and positions. The images also change in pretty good transitions which are eye catching and may make your lock screen cooler.

Just turn 'On' the slide show switch and the following settings would popup:

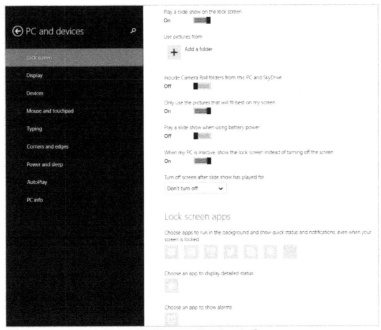

Figure 67: Slide Show Setting on the Lock Screen

The explanation of each is given below:

# Use Pictures from – Pictures

If you do not want to use Pictures, press / click this button and in the resulting popup, press Remove Button. This option will be closed.

# Add a Folder

If you want to save the images to be used, specifically, for the pictures, press the button with '+' sign and a new folder will be added in your PC where you can save your images.

Figure 68: Add a Folder

# Include Camera Roll Folders from this PC and SkyDrive

Turning 'On' this Switch will include your camera roll for the image selection for the Lock Scree.

Figure 69: Include Camera Roll from This PC

**NOTE**

Following Switches in this Section are set 'On' / 'Off' by Default:

Play a Slide Show on Lock Screen: Off
Include Camera Roll Folders.....Off
Only Use the Pictures............On
Play a Slide Show When Using.....Off
When my Pc is inactive, show.On
Turn off screen after slide show
Don't Turn Off

# Only Use the Pictures that Fits Best for My Screen

By turning On this switch, the Windows will use only those pictures from your PC for the Lock Screen which are best for the PC of your Screen. All the rest will not be used for the purpose.

Only use the pictures that will fit best on my screen

On

Figure 70: Selection of Best Pictures

# Play a Slide Chow When Using Battery Power

As the slide show on the screen of your PC consumes a lot of power of your PC battery, you are given option to turn On or Off this switch.

Figure 71: Play a Slide Show When Using Battery

# When the PC is Inactive, Show the Lock Screen .......

Some of the people do not like to turn off the PC while they are busy in some other task. So, if they do not want to turn off the screen while it is inactive, turn On this screen or otherwise turn Off this Switch.

When my PC is inactive, show the lock screen instead of turning off the screen

On

Figure 72: Display of Lock Screen When PC is Inactive

# Turn Off the Screen After the Slide Show has Played for

This option is set to turn On and set the time for the slide show for the limited time.

Press to Set Turn Off Screen after some Time

Figure 73: Turn Off Screen Setting before Drop Down

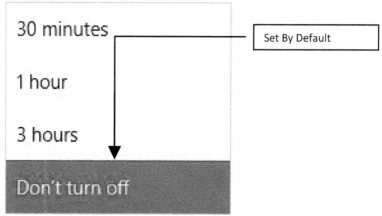

Figure 74: Drop Down Menu

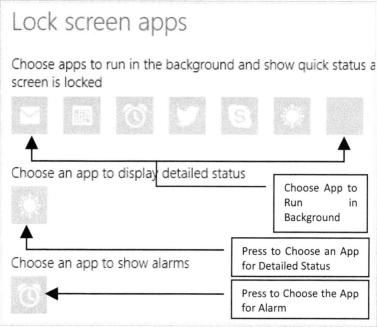

Figure 75: Lock Screen Apps

Following options are available for the users to select from:

# Lock Screen Apps

Immediately below the settings for the slide show (see above section), the 3 sections are given about the Lock Screen apps.

Let's have a close look at each of the options:

# Choose Apps to Run in Background

· · · · · · ·

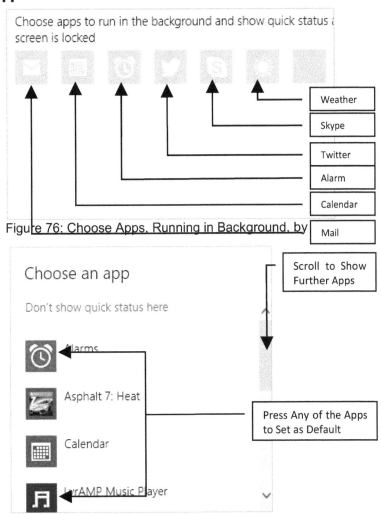

Figure 76: Choose Apps, Running in Background, by

Figure 77: Press Any App to Run in Background

Pressing any of the apps will display a popup, displaying a message and further selection; Don't show quick status here. Upon selecting any app will remove its status from here.

This option will provide you the chance to select the display of app notifications on specified location on lock screen.

There are seven different standard locations to show app notifications and 1 location to show detailed notifications from an app. You also get the option to show 1 alarm app notifications on a separate location.

Apps set by Default are:

1. Mail
2. Calendar
3. Alarm
4. Weather

It would also display the quick status and notifications, even when your screen is locked.

If you want to choose an app, press + which would open up a pop up, asking you to choose an app, which will display notifications on lock screen.

# Choose an App to Display Detailed Status

Upon pressing this button, you will see a popup.

Figure 78: Choose an App to Show Detailed Status For Weather

Here, you can select an app to give you detailed status. You can select only one app but you can change it at will.

# Choose an App to Show Alarms

Press the button in this option to select an app to show Alarms.

**NOTE**

Alarm App is set by Default.

Choose an app to show alarms

Figure 79: Choosing an App to Give Detailed Status for alarm

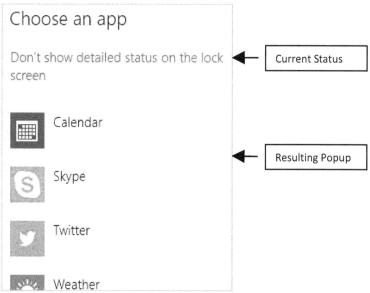

Choose an app

Don't show detailed status on the lock ← Current Status
screen

Calendar

Skype

Twitter                    ← Resulting Popup

Weather

Figure 80: Selecting an App to Choose Alarm App

Pressing 'Choose an app to show alarms' will result in a popup' displaying a message from Windows, as displayed in Figure 66.

# Camera

Windows 8.1 also includes an awesome feature to access the Camera app right from the lock screen and don't even need to unlock your PC and launch camera app.

This option can be very helpful for people who love to capture special moments using their Windows 8.1 device and still don't want to miss those moments.

## NOTE

The switch to use the camera is On by Default.

To use the camera, even when your PC is locked, swipe down on the lock screen.

# Enabling Camera Access from Lock Screen

To enable the PC to use the camera from the lock screen, just change the switch option to On under PC & devices > Lock Screen and Camera section

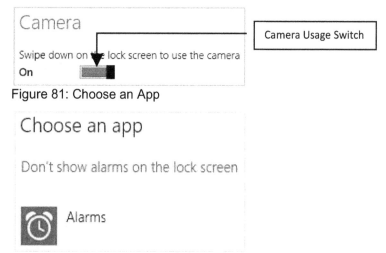

Figure 81: Choose an App

.Figure 82: Allowing the Windows 8.1 to Use Camera in Lock Screen

# PC and Devices – Display

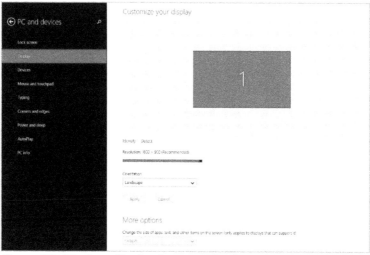

Figure 83: Display - Customize your Display

Display options in PC Settings holds the options like screen resolutions, screen selection, screen behavior and the screen orientation.

# Customize your Display

Here, you will be provided the option to optimize the display of your PC and would give you the option like set screen resolutions, orientations and more.

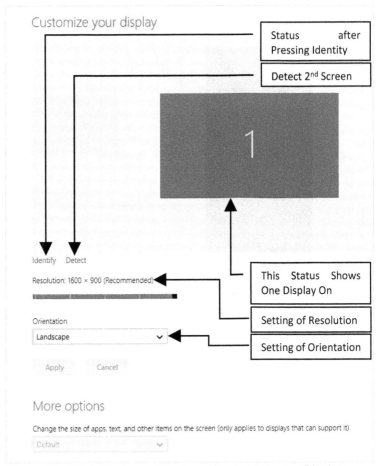

Figure 84: PC & Devices - Display - Customize your Display

# Identify

This option becomes useful when you connect two or more screens to your PC and wants to see which screen is acting as which one.

Figure 85: Identify the Display

# Detect

On my Pc when I pressed Detect option, the resultant message is displayed below:

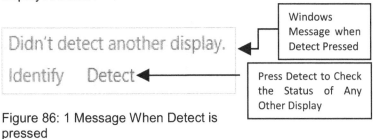

Figure 86: 1 Message When Detect is pressed

# Resolution

This switch lets you select your screen resolution from a bunch of options.

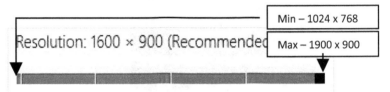

Figure 87: Resolution Setting Slider

The slider switch can be moved left or right to select from different resolutions but, the slider maybe disabled if, you don't have a capable graphic card.

Some common screen resolutions are:

1024 x 768
1152 x 864
1280 x 768
1280 x 800
1366 x 768
1600 x 900
1920 x 1080

**NOTE**

The resolutions provided may differ from PC to PC due to hardware changes.

You need to install the appropriate graphics driver for your PC to get full graphics acceleration with maximum screen resolutions.

# Orientation

The Orientation option lets you select the orientation of your screen where you can select from different screen orientations like landscape and portrait etc.

Figure 88: Orientation Setting

By pressing the drop down menu, following options will appear in the popup from where you may select Orientation of your choice:

Orientation

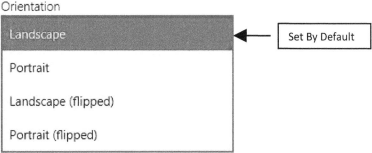

Figure 89: Options to Set the Orientation of PC

# Portrait

If you opt to change the orientation of the display, from the default to the, for example, portrait, by pressing the Apply, your screen size will be changed, immediately.

Here you will be asked a question:

➢ Keep these display settings and will be asked to respond in 15 second, after which the previous settings will be restored.

**NOTE**

This option can also be used to configure the orientation of your tablet PC if, you have turned-off the auto rotation of screen.

If you want to keep the changes, press the Keep the Changes otherwise press the Revert.

In addition to it, you are also given the option to set the size of the apps.

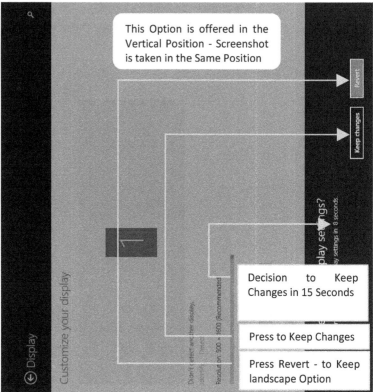

Figure 90: Orientation Changes – Portrait Option

# Landscape (Flipped)

Now, if you want to customize your display to next orientation option, i.e. Landscape (Flipped), press the option and see the screenshot here.

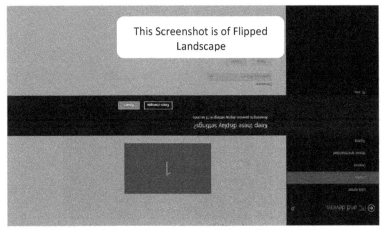

Figure 91: Orientation - Landscape (Flipped)

# Bluetooth

In the Bluetooth option, you will be asked; whether you want other Bluetooth devices to detect your PC or not. You may switch On the option by sliding switch to left or right.

If you switch On Bluetooth and some other device(s) is in range, you would be asked to pair with that device by providing a pin code.

You would be provided a pin code which you need to enter on your device to pair it with your PC.

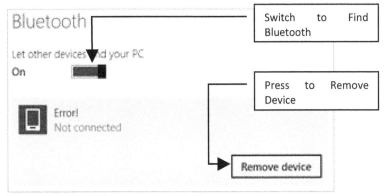

Figure 92: Blue Tooth Device Setting

99

# PC & Devices – Devices

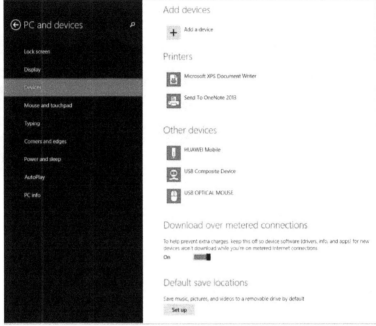

Figure 93: Devices Setting

Devices tab in the PC Settings holds the options to add or remove devices which are connected to your PC. Here you are also shown all the devices which are currently connected to your PC.

Let us have a close look on each of the options available here.

# Add or Remove

Here you can add a device by clicking a big sign button with image of '+' which will search out the new devices, attached to your PC and will install appropriate software for the device.

100

Figure 94: Add New Device

In my PC, I received the response, given below, when I click the '+' button of Add a Device. Other PCs may receive differing response, depending upon the specs of the PC.

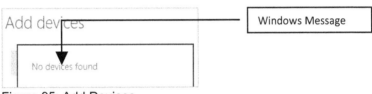

Figure 95: Add Devices

# Printers

Here the printers menu is separate from other devices where all the connected printers and print capable devices are shown.

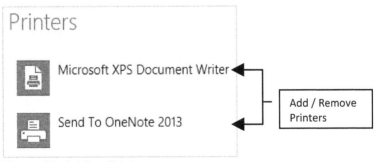

Figure 96: Adding Printers

You can also remove a printer from the list of devices by pressing it and tapping the 'Remove device' button.

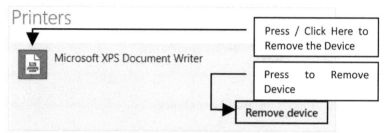

Figure 97: Add or Remove (Change) Printers

Figure 98: Settings of Other Devices

# Other Devices

Other devices option lets you see the other connected devices of your PC where anything from mobile device to a mouse and webcam etc. can be seen.

You can also remove the device of your choice by pressing its names and then, 'Remove device' button.

Other devices

HUAWEI Mobile

Press Here to Remove the Device

USB Composite Device

Remove device

USB OPTICAL MOUSE

Figure 99: Removing the Device from PC

# Download Over Metered Connections

This is very interesting, yet very useful and important option, given to the users, who are otherwise using very expensive and metered Internet connections.

Download over metered connection

Turn    On    the Download    Metered Connection

To help prevent extra charges, keep this off so device software devices won't download while you're on metered Internet conn

On

Figure 100: Download over Metered Connections

If you want to avoid, downloading the software(s), such as, drivers, info and app, while you are on metered Internet connections where each MB of download costs you, use this option. Just slide right the switch to On or to the left to Off.

# Default Save Locations

If you want to save your files to any removable drive or device, just press 'Set up' and you would be able to select the device to save files and the PC will save all the files to this drive by default.

Figure 101: Saving Music, Pictures and Videos in a Removable Device

Upon pressing the Set up button, a popup would display. Your PC may have different Setting popup.

As described in the popup, a folders would be created by the Windows to save your music, pictures and videos.

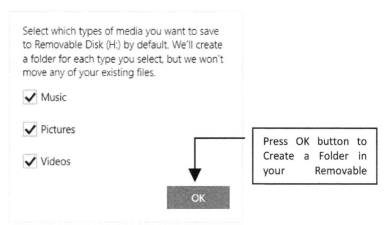

Figure 102: Creation of a Folder for Music, Pictures & Videos

# PC & Devices - Mouse & Touch Pad

On this window, designed for Mouse and Touchpad settings, you will be given options about the Mouse and Touchpad, separately.

Figure 103: PC & Devices - Mouse & Touchpad

# Mouse

The first question will be asked about the selection of the primary button of the Mouse and will be asked to select from the scroll down option of Left or Right.

# Selecting the Primary Button

Pressing / clicking the drop down menu, a menu would appear, displaying 2 options to select one from them giving you the option to select one of your choice and desire:

**NOTE**

Windows 8.1 default return message upon clicking the Set Up button will be; 'Connect removable device and try again'.

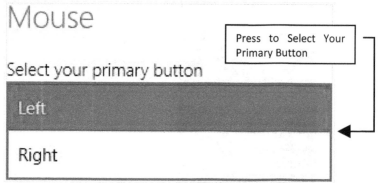

Figure 104: Setting your Primary Button

# Rolling the Mouse Wheel to Scroll

Here, you will be asked one option to select from the two given:

1. Multiple Lines at a Time
2. One Screen at a Time

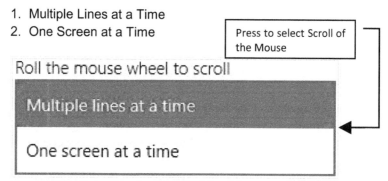

Figure 105: Selecting the Scroll of the Mouse

# Selecting the Number of Lines per Scroll

If you select first option of selecting the Multiple Lines at a Time, a slider will be enabled below the option, from where you may select the number of lines to scroll each time. This option will select from 1 – 100 line per scroll.

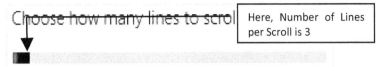

Figure 106: Selection of Lines per Scroll of Mouse

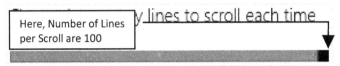

Figure 107: Selection of Lines per Scroll of Mouse

# Touch Pad

As the Windows 8.1 is, specifically, developed for the touch screen devices, such as, tablet PCs, touchpad is specifically highlighted. As the cursor may be moved, accidentally, while typing, you are advised to change the delay in moving the cursor. For the purpose, you are given the 4 options of delay.

Just press / click the drop down menu and the options popup will be opened.

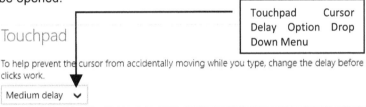

Figure 108: Touchpad Cursor Delay Option Setter

As displayed in the Figure 78, the drop down menu offers 4 different delay options:

# NOTE

Medium Delay is Set by Default.

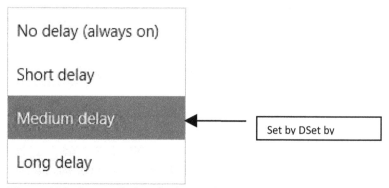

Figure 109: Cursor Delay Option in Touchpad

1. No Delay (*Always On*)
2. Short Delay
3. Medium Delay
4. Long Delay

# PC and Devices – Typing

The next addition in the PC Settings is the options about the Typing.

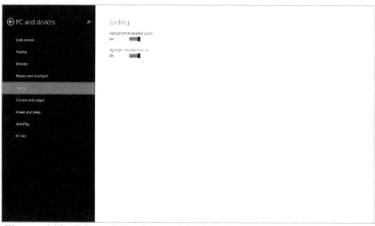

Figure 110: PC and Devices – Typing

# Autocorrect Misspelled Words

Windows 8.1 includes a built-in grammar which checks your sentences and words for grammatical mistakes. Windows will autocorrect the mistakes as well if you have enabled the option.

Figure 111: Autocorrect Switch

Just turn On the switch to autocorrect misspelled words option enabled.

Figure 112: Highlight Misspelled Words Option

# Highlight Misspelled Words

You can enable the autocorrect of words by moving the slider switch to the right and Windows will also highlight the misspelled words if, you have enabled the option.

**NOTE**

Spelling and Highlighted Misspelled Word is Set On by Default.

# Corners and Edges

Windows 8.1 just like Windows 8 includes hot corners which lets you perform some quick app specific tasks like app switching and app snap etc. Hot Corners are also the source to access the Charms Bar and Start from apps.

# App Switching

Figure 113: PC and Devices - Corners and Edges

# Allowing the Switching between Recent Apps

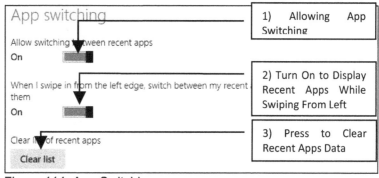

Figure 114: App Switching

This switch option lets you choose whether the most recently opened apps can be resumed right from where you left when you close the app or navigate away from it.

# Display of Recent Apps While Swiping from Left Edge

This options lets you choose whether the recently closed apps can be accessed by swiping from left or not. It is very helpful while you are multi-tasking and using multiple apps at a time.

## NOTE

All 4 Switches are Turned On in Corner & Edges Section by Default.

# Clear Loss of Recent Apps

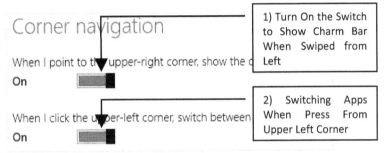

Corner navigation

When I point to the upper-right corner, show the c

On

1) Turn On the Switch to Show Charm Bar When Swiped from Left

When I click the upper-left corner, switch between

On

2) Switching Apps When Press From Upper Left Corner

Figure 115: Corner Navigation

If you want to clear the list of app, just press the Clear button. And that's all!

# PC and Devices – Corner Navigation

Option of display of search, share, start, devices and setting, starts when you point to the upper – top right corner.

Windows 8.1 includes a quick access menu for all basic functions of Windows; named as Charms Bar. The Charms Bar can be accessed by moving the mouse cursor down from top right corner of screen but, for some users, it may cause problems as Charms keep popping up. Microsoft has provided the solution for that problem and you can switch the Charms bar access from top right corner by turning this switch on.

It display the recently open apps whenever the mouse cursor touches the upper – left corner.

Windows 8.1 lets you switch to the most recent apps by swiping from right and if you move your mouse cursor to top left corner, you will see a whole list of recently access apps.

You can easily disable that list by enabling this option if, you don't want to see that list anymore.

# PC and Devices – Power & Sleep

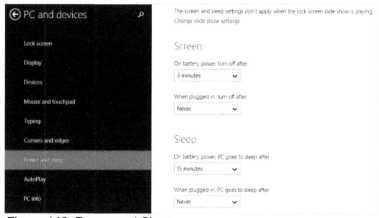

Figure 116: Power and Sleep

This window in the PC Settings holds the options related to the power settings of your PC. The options which previously could be found 'Power Options' on desktop Control Panel have now been moved to the PC Settings.

# Screen

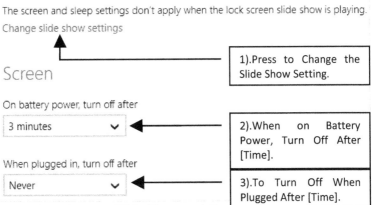

Figure 117: Change Slide Show and Screen

# On Battery Power, Turn Off After

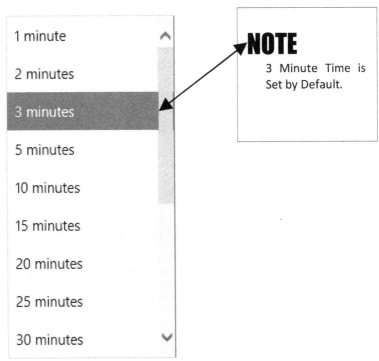

Figure 118: When On Battery, Turn Off after Time

This option lets you control the behavior of your PC's screen when you are running it on battery power.

As the screen and sleep timing are directly affected by the slide show, to change the slide show setting, press the change slide show setting.

# When Plugged in, turn off after

You can select different timings, from 1 minute to 5 hours to turn off the display of the screen to save battery.

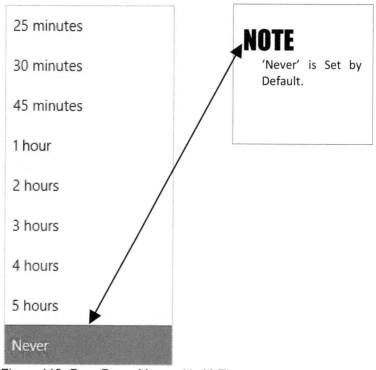

Figure 119: Drop Down Menu with 16 Times

Simply, press the drop down menu and set the time to turn down battery in the popup.

# Sleep

For setting during the Sleep, two options are available in Windows 8.1 as displayed.

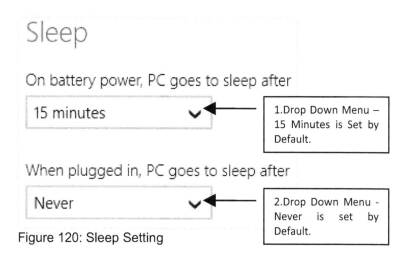

Figure 120: Sleep Setting

# On Battery Power, PC Goes to Sleep After

You can control whether and when your PC goes to sleep while being operated on battery power. This option can be useful to improve the battery timing of your PC.

Upon pressing the drop down menu, a popup will appear with 16 time options, starting with 1 Minute to 5 hours and Never. You may select any time, depending upon your need.

115

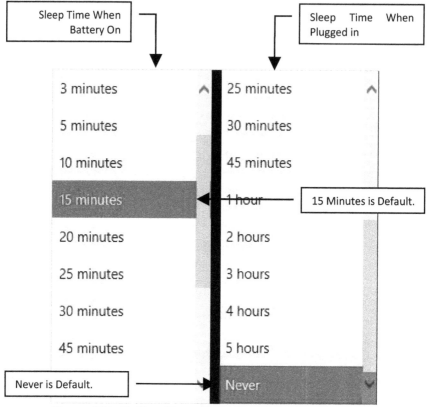

Figure 121: Setting Sleep Time when on Battery Power

# When plugged in, PC Goes to Sleep After

You can also control whether your PC goes to sleep when you have plugged it to a power source.

Press the drop down menu to open the popup, showing the 'Sleep time when plugged in'. Here select the time from 16 time options and 1 Never options as per your desired settings.

# PC and Devices - AutoPlay

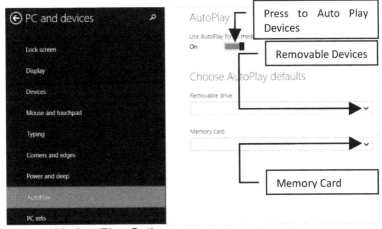

Figure 122: AutoPlay Options

In the AutoPlay window, you will be given the option to use AutoPlay for all media and devices or not by switching between On / Off.

# Use AutoPlay for Media & Devices

Figure 123: AutoPlay Options Switch

Just turn On the AutoPlay switch and the autoplay will be enabled on your PC.

# Choose AutoPlay Defaults
## *Removable Drive*

In this option, you will be asked to opt about the Removable Drives by asking to respond to the following 4 options:

117

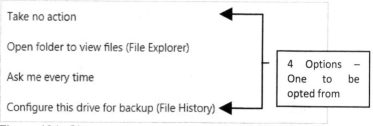

Figure 124: Choosing Auto Play Device

- Take No Action
- Open Folder to View Files (File Explorer)
- Ask Every Time
- Configure this Drive for Backup (File History).

This option can be helpful when you want to select a specific behavior for all your removable devices when they are connected to your PC.

# Memory Card

About the memory card, 6 following different options (It are in your PC while options in your PC may be different, depending upon the configuration of your PC) will be offered:

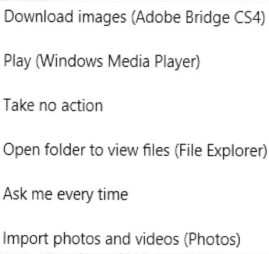

Figure 125: Choosing AutoPlay Defaults - Memory Card

- Download Images (Adobe Bridge CS4)
- Play (Windows Media Player)
- Take no Action
- Open Folder to View Files (File Explorer)
- Ask me Every Time
- Import photos and videos (Photos)

Here you can select the default behavior of the memory card which are inserted in your PC like play the content of card, download images, or import photos or videos from the card.

**NOTE**

Nothing is Set by Default.

# PC Info

PC Info tab of Windows 8.1 in PC Settings shows all the information which could, previously, be seen in the 'System' page of desktop.

Here you are shown the information like your PC name, hardware specifications, Windows details including the editions and the activation details.

You can also change the product key of your PC from this page and rename your PC as well.

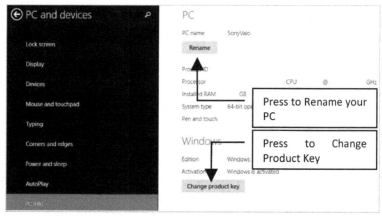

Figure 126: PC Info

You can also change the product key of your PC from this page and rename your PC.

120

**CHAPTER 6** »»

# Managing Accounts

Accounts page in the PC Settings holds the options related to the user accounts and their options of Windows 8.1.

Figure 127: PC Settings – Accounts

# Your Account

In your account window, first of all your name and our email is shown if you have connected your Microsoft account with it.

# Disconnect

To Disconnect Online Account, Press

Figure 128: Disconnect Option

Pressing this option will take to the next windows where you will be given further option, given below:

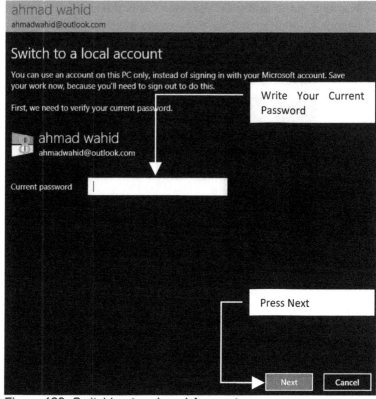

Figure 129: Switching to a Local Account

Upon pressing the Disconnect, the next window will take you to the window where you will be asked to write your current password to press next button.

It would take you to the next windows where your local account setting options will be enquired upon to switch On to the next account.

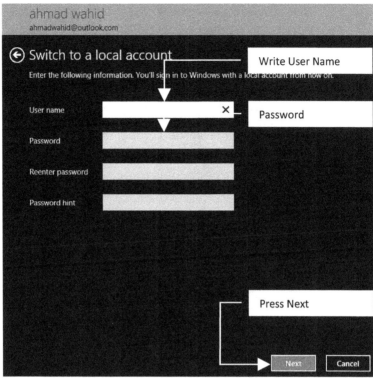

Figure 130: Switching On to the Local Account

# More Online Accounts Settings

More account settings online

Figure 131: More Online Account Settings

Upon pressing the more account settings Online, Windows will open up your Microsoft Online Outlook, Hotmail or the concerned account. See URL in Footnote. [2]

---

Here you will be asked to log on to your account and make necessary changes in your account, such as, password or other account settings.

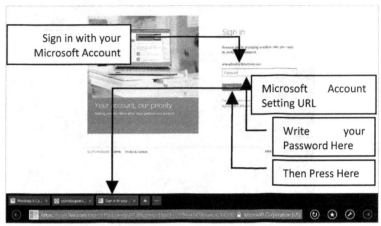

Figure 132: Sign in to Your Online Account

# Account Picture

If you want to change your account picture, just press Browse button and the options to change your account picture will appear. It would help you to choose the picture, either from your own PC or from some other source.

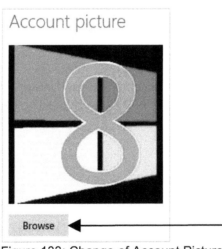

Figure 133: Change of Account Picture

Pressing the Browse will take you to the window with pictures from where you can select the picture of your choice.

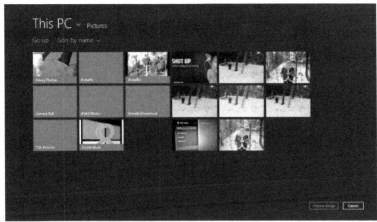

Figure 134: Changing Pictures for your Account

# Create an Account Picture

In Create an account pictures for your account, you are given 2 options:

> ➤ Create and Account by Taking Camera Snap
> ➤ Selecting picture from People app

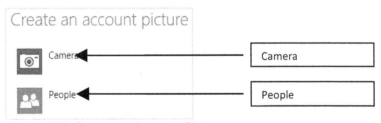

Figure 135: Create an Account Picture

# Camera

By pressing the Camera button, the camera app will be opened, helping you to take snaps for your account picture.

# People

Alternatively, pressing the People button will take you to the People App where you may Change Your Account picture and other details.

Pressing the People button will open up the change window where you may change / amend the account pictures.

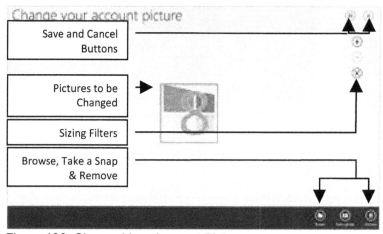

Figure 136: Change Your Account Pictures

Pressing Browse button will take you again to your PC.

# Sign in Options

This tab of Account page in PC Settings of Windows 8.1 lets you choose the sign-in behavior of your Windows where you can select from a couple of sign-in options.

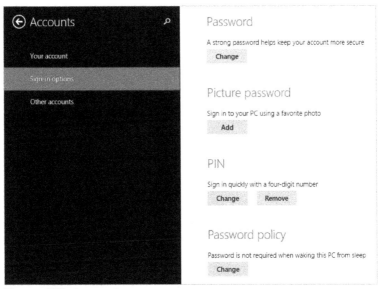

Figure 137: Accounts

Let's have a closer look upon each of the options.

# Password

This option lets you change the password of your user account.

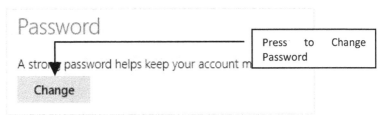

Figure 138: Change Password

The change password will open, depending upon the type of account you are using, e.g. Microsoft account or a local account.

Figure 139: Sign in to Your Microsoft Account

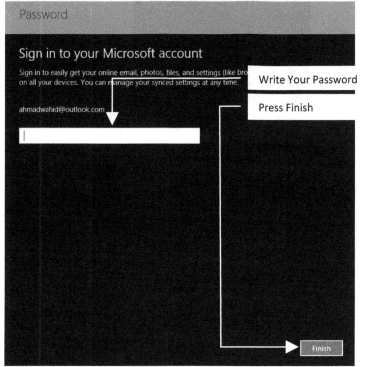

Figure 140: Change Picture Password

# Picture Password

Signing in to PC by using your favorite Photo as picture password where you have to draw three different patterns on the image in-order to unlock your PC.

# Pin

You can also use 4 digit pin code to use as sign-in option.

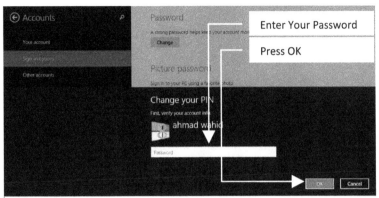

Figure 141: Adding 4 Digit PIN

Just press Change button and change your PIN popup will open.

Figure 142: Change Your PIN

Here, you are required to first verify your password by entering your password.

Pressing OK will a new popup window where you are required to Change your PIN. Enter your 4 digit PIN. Twice, and press Finish, the option to use PIN code to log in will become default.

131

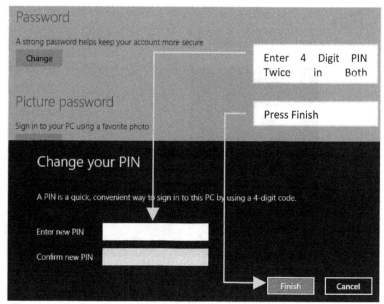

Figure 143: Changing the PIN Option

# Password Policy

This option lets you choose whether you can sign-in to the PC without providing a password when the PC is being awaked from sleep.

By default, you are required to awake your PC from sleep and this message is displayed in Sign in section, i.e. 'Password is required when waking this PC from sleep'.

Figure 144: Password Policy

132

Simply, pressing Change button will allow anyone to wake this PC without a password.

Immediately after pressing Change button, the resulting message is presented in Figure 114.

**NOTE**

Enabling this option is not recommended since, anyone can access your PC. If you lock PC and your PC goes to sleep during that password.

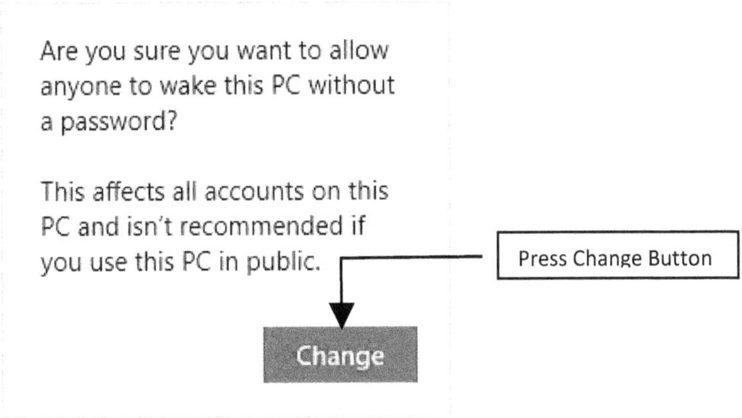

Are you sure you want to allow anyone to wake this PC without a password?

This affects all accounts on this PC and isn't recommended if you use this PC in public.

Press Change Button

Change

Figure 145: Awaking This PC without Password

Upon pressing Change button, the resulting message in the Password policy will be change, i.e. 'Password is not required when waking this PC from sleep'.

Figure 146: Awaking Without Password Enabled

# Other Accounts

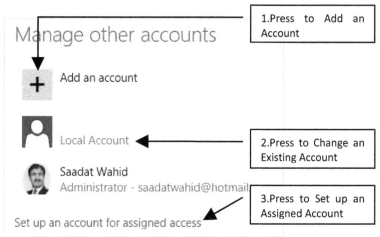

Figure 147: Manage Your Other Accounts

# Add a User

This tab prides you options to add or edit existing user accounts of this PC.

Press '+' to 'Add an account' to add a new user account. It would open up a popup. Here you will be asked to give the Microsoft email address of the new account.

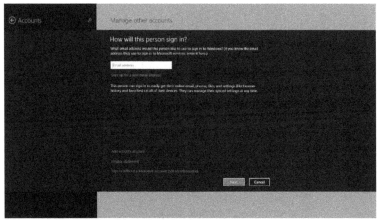

Figure 148: Adding New Account

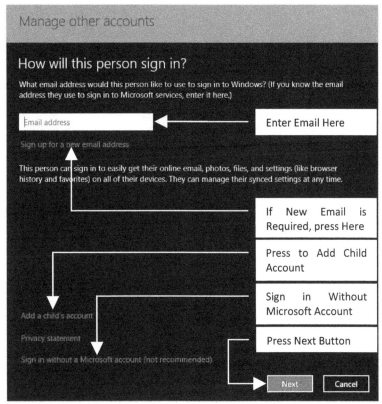

Figure 149: Adding New Account

# Add a User – Sign Up for the New Email Address

If the Microsoft Account is not available, sign up for a new email address which will open us a new popup. Here you may add a new Microsoft account for the new user of the Windows 8.1.

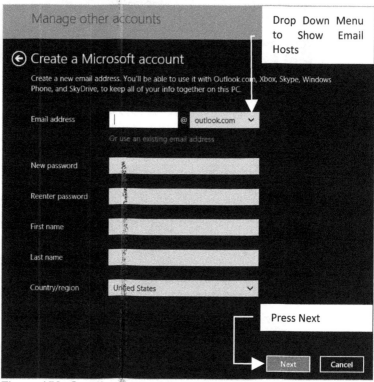

Figure 150: Creating a new Microsoft Account

Fill up the popup form and new Microsoft account will be created which will help to add a new account.

# Set up An Account for An Assigned Access

You are also given an option to set up an account for assigned access. Just press the Set up an assign ......... The new popup window will give you 2 options.

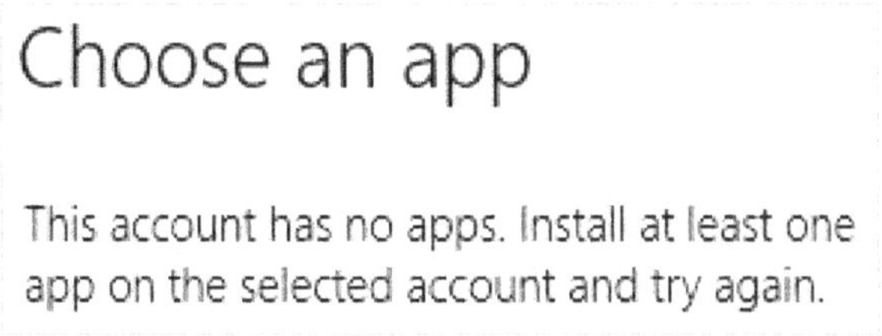

# Choose an app

This account has no apps. Install at least one
app on the selected account and try again.

Figure 151: Setting up and Account for the Assigned Access

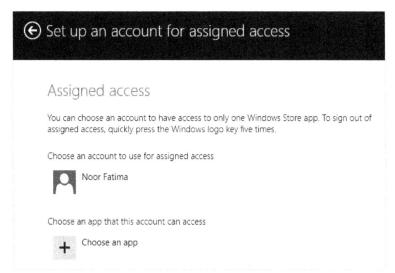

Figure 152: Choosing an Account for Assigning Access

Here, you will asked to choose any account from the existing ones but with message that you must restart your PC to apply the changes

Figure 153: Choosing a App for Assign Access

.

Here, in This PC, it is informed to me that as this account has no apps, install at least one app on the account and try again.

# Adding Child's Account

Windows 8.1 also provides you an option to add Child's account. Just press the 'Add a Child's Account' and a new popup will appear.

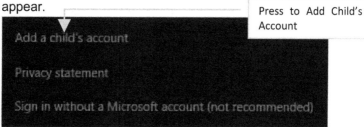

Figure 154: Adding a Child's Account

Here, enter the email address of the child. If the child do not have the email address, Sign up for a new email address of child.

Alternatively, press the option to add a child's account with email address.

If the child do not have the email account, you would be taken to the window with the account opening info.

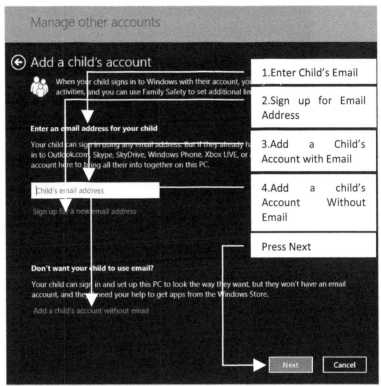

Figure 155: Adding a Child's Account

If the child do not have the email account, you would be taken to the window with the account opening info.

Pressing the 'Add a child's account without email' will take you to a new popup.

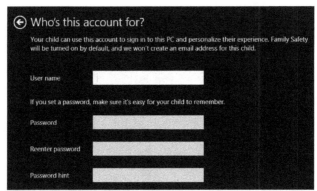

Figure 156: This Account if For Whom

When you would complete the form, click the Next button and it would take you to the next window. Pressing Finish button will take you to the window where all the active accounts will be displayed.

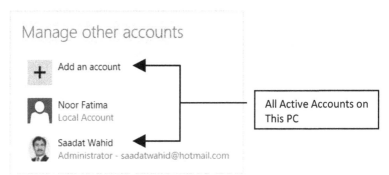

Figure 157: All Active Accounts on This PC

# Privacy Statement

This option will take you to the 'Windows 8 and Windows Server 2012 Privacy Statement' at the site of Microsoft Windows.[3].

---

3        http://windows.microsoft.com/en-US/windows-8/windows-8-privacy-statement?ocid=W8_UI.

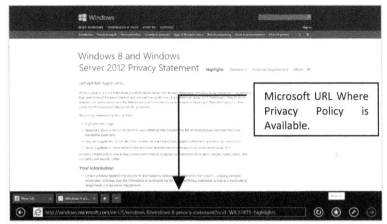

Figure 158: Microsoft URL Where Privacy Policy is Available

# Adding a User without the Microsoft Account

At this window, you may add a new person to use this PC either with a Microsoft Account or with a Local Account where you will be required to provide the details about user name, password, password hint etc.

Upon pressing the 'Sign in without Microsoft Account' the popup window will offer 2 option for the purpose.

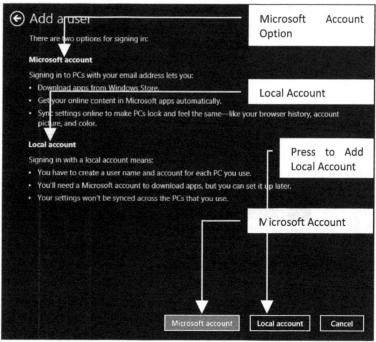

Figure 159: Add a User without Microsoft Account

# Editing the Account Type

You can also edit the user account type from this tab.

**NOTE**

Adding an user without Microsoft Account is not liked by Microsoft.

Simply press the user account you want to edit and you will either get the option to edit the account type or remove that user.

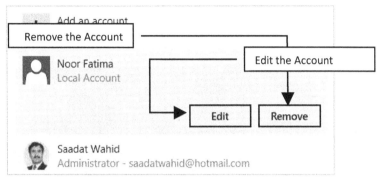
Figure 160: Editing an Existing Account

Pressing the Edit will take you to the Edit page, letting you change the user account type.

Previously, the account is set as the standard user by Default.

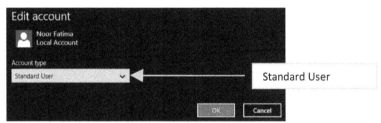
Figure 161: Account Type - Standard User

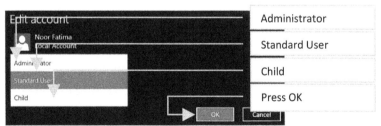
Figure 162: Edit Account

# Remove

The remove options asks for confirmation to delete and on pressing the 'Delete account and data' will permanently delete that account and all the data associated with it.

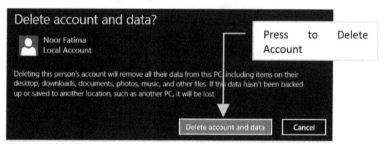

Figure 163: Deleting Account and Data

**CHAPTER 7**

# Unlocking the PC

The first thing appearing before you, after boot of Windows 8.1, is the Lock Screen. Just like Windows 8, you can customize your lock screen according to your own choice and needs.

You can select different images or slide shows, displayed notifications or detailed notifications from apps right on the Lock Screen.

Windows 8.1 also has also included the option to access Camera right from your Lock Screen.

Windows 8.1 presents following two different options to set up Lock Screen images:

1.      Still Background
2.      Picture frame slide show

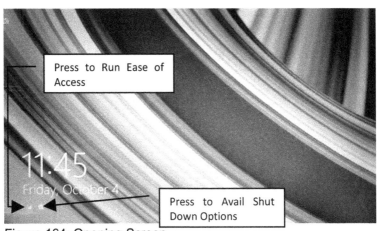

Figure 164: Opening Screen

You can choose from any given 'still images' as the Lock Screen but that must be of at least 1024 x 768 pixels. We can set Lock Screen by one of the following:

1.  Top Settings from PC Settings
➢  Go to Lock Screen
➢  Select any still image as background.

# Using Slide Show as Lock Screen Image

Alternatively, you can also use slide show as lock screen image, displaying different images on your lock screen in random order and sizes.

# Lock Screen Notifications

Windows 8.1 Lock Screen, like Windows 8, also has the option to display notifications on Lock Screen but Windows 8.1 displays more detailed notifications.

In Windows 8.1, you can now select the app, displaying the detailed notifications from option of customization. Now, more options like the Alarms on Lock Screen are also available.

# Camera Access from Lock Screen

**Option to Access Camera Right from Your Lock Screen**: The best and probably the most awesome addition in the Lock Screen of Windows 8.1 is the ability to access the Camera app, right from your Lock Screen.

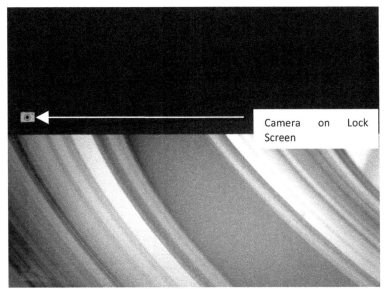

Camera on Lock Screen

Figure 165: Camera on Lock Screen

So, if you have some place where you immediately have to access your Camera to take snap, you don't have to sign-in to your Windows but, now, you can directly open the Camera app from your Lock Screen without unlocking it.

Once you are on the Lock Screen, simply swipe down the Lock Screen and your Camera app will be opened for you to start taking snaps.

This option to access camera isn't enabled by default but, you can enable it by going to PC Setting.

# Unlocking the PC

Windows 8.1 just like Windows 8 provides you three different options to unlock and sign-in to your PC.

Let us have a look on each of the 3 unlock options.

# Password Sign-in

The first and the default option to unlock your PC is the password. You simply have to type the password which you selected while installing Windows 8.1 and your PC would be unlocked.

Figure 166: Picture Password

# Picture Password

The second option to unlock your PC is the picture password where you have to draw three different patterns on the image you selected to unlock your PC.

# NOTE

Password may either be your Microsoft account password or local one selected during post-installation of Windows.

Picture password isn't enabled by default but, you can enable it by going to PC Settings.

150

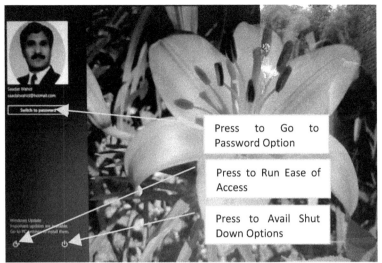

Figure 167: Opening Windows with Picture Password

# PIN

Windows 8.1 also provides the option to use 4 digit pin code as the sign-in option to open your PC.

Figure 168: PIN Password

The four digit code is best for people who want quick login access to their Windows PC.

**CHAPTER 8**

# Storage at SkyDrive

Windows 8.1 is the first ever OS by Microsoft which includes deep SkyDrive integration. The cloud storage by Microsoft is now the base for file storage and backup of Windows 8.1.

Figure 169: SkyDrive

Under SkyDrive page in PC Settings, you will get the following three options with each having its own sections and configuration settings.

1. Storage Space
2. Files
3. Sync Setting

**NOTE**

For the purpose, you must enable the SkyDrive integration.

# Storage Space

When you press the Storage Space option of the SkyDrive, you will be provided following information about the facility of the storage space, available on SkyDrive by Microsoft:

# Your Storage Space on SkyDrive

1. Storage Limit: For the starters, it is 7.00 GB but, it may be more for paid subscribers.
2. Available Storage
3. Used Storage
4. The current percentage status of the usage of your SkyDrive

Figure 170: Storage Space

# Buy More Storage

The Option to Buy More Storage which is as follows:

20 GB   / $10.00 per year
50 GB   / $25.00 per year
100 GB / $50.00 per year

In my PC this is displayed on a slider as shown in the Figure above.

Upon pressing But a popup on the internet would appear as given below:

Figure 170: Buy a SkyDrive Storage Plan

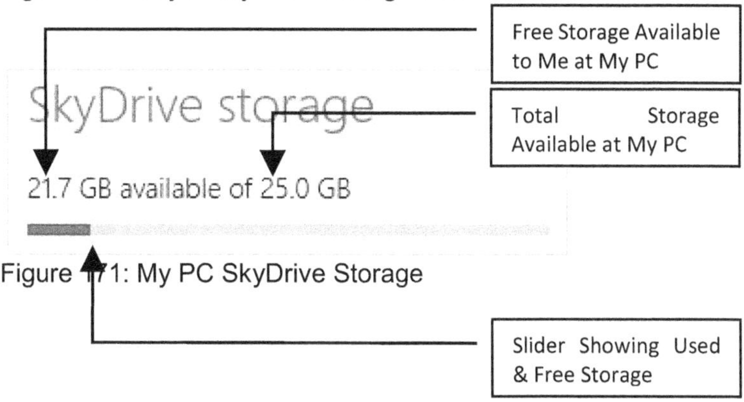

SkyDrive storage ——————— Free Storage Available to Me at My PC

————— Total Storage Available at My PC

21.7 GB available of 25.0 GB

Figure 171: My PC SkyDrive Storage

————— Slider Showing Used & Free Storage

# Saving the Documents on SkyDrive by Default

If you want to save your documents on SkyDrive by Default, turn On this switch.

**NOTE**

'See my files on SkyDrive' link opens up the SkyDrive app where you can view all the files you have stored on your cloud *storage.*

Save File on SkyDrive by Default Switch

Figure 172: Saving Docs on SkyDrive by Default

# See My Files on SkyDrive

When you press the 'See my files on SkyDrive' option, following arrangement of documents on SkyDrive and This PC will be shown.

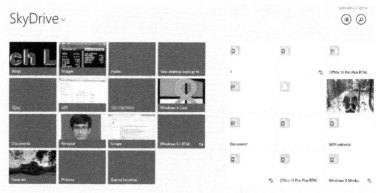

Figure 173: My Files on SkyDrive and This PC

# SkyDrive - Camera Roll Folder

If you have switched On the option to upload videos to your SkyDrive and your PC uploads still photos, screenshots and videos to SkyDrive folders right from your Camera Roll, you have the option to get and retrieve any of them from any device. Further, you may get to your SkyDrive folder from anywhere on the Globe.

Figure 174: Upload Photos and Videos

Windows informs you that higher quality photos, screenshots and videos may take more space and longer time to upload on the SkyDrive.

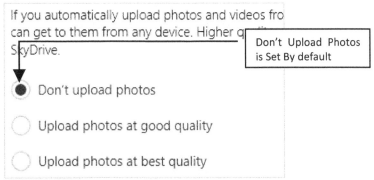

Figure 175: Options to Upload Photos and Videos on SkyDrive

You are provided three different options for photo uploading provided you enable them.

➢ Don't upload photos
➢ Upload photos at good quality
➢ Upload photos at best quality

159

# Automatically Upload Videos by Default

Turning On the switch, will start uploading all your videos on SkyDrive by Default.

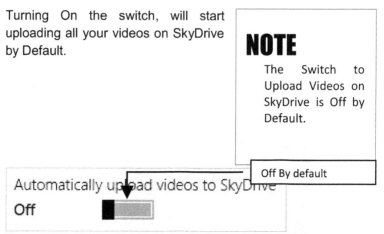

**NOTE**

The Switch to Upload Videos on SkyDrive is Off by Default.

Off By default

Automatically upload videos to SkyDrive

Off

Figure 176: Automatically Upload Videos to SkyDrive

# Sync Settings

The next setting about the SkyDrive over the PC settings are about Sync Setting.

Windows 8.1 saves your files, settings, personalization and app settings to the cloud using your Microsoft account and same settings can be secured on other devices connected, using the same Microsoft account.

**NOTE**

Sync setting switch on this PC is On by default while the question about the back-up settings, not synced are Off.

All the settings related to your sync of Windows 8 can be controlled from this Tab.

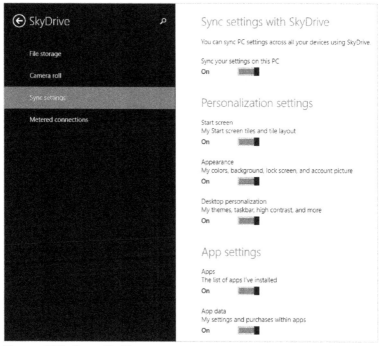

Figure 177: Sync Setting

# Sync

Offering us two switch options about the sync setting on your PC, Microsoft informed us that all your devices can be set to sync, using SkyDrive along with those setting which you don't sync.
Two switch options about your permission to allow the sync on your PC are:

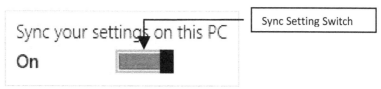

Figure 178: Sync Setting with SkyDrive

# Sync settings on this PC

The switch in above Figure is main switch of all the other settings of the page where you can turn On / Off the sync completely.

# Back up Settings that are Not Synced

This option lets you select whether the settings which can't be synced are backed up by Windows 8 or not.

# Personalization Setting

This section lets you control the sync settings related to the personalization of Windows and its different parts.

# Start Screen

Windows 8.1 is very easy to personalize and the Start Screen of Windows 8.1.

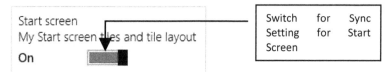

Figure 179: Start Screen Setting

It can be customized according to your desire by resizing app tiles, making groups and naming them. All these settings can also be saved to the cloud storage and same settings will be set on other device connected to same Microsoft account.

**NOTE**

All the 3 Personalization setting switches on this PC are On by default.

162

# Appearance

This option lets you control whether the colorization of Windows, the background pattern, lock screen image and the account picture of your account are synced or not.

Figure 180: Appearance Setting

# Desktop Personalization

Figure 181: Desktop Personalization

This option lets you control the sync behavior of desktop options like themes, taskbar settings, high contrast themes, desktop colorization etc.

# **App Setting**

App settings are also synced from your PC to the cloud storage where different apps related things are synced.

# Installed Apps

This option lets you select the list of apps installed on this PC are synced to the cloud so that you may know which app is installed on which PC.

Figure 182: Installed Apps

# Other Settings

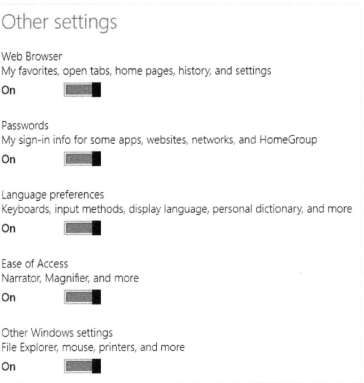

Figure 183: Other Settings

Other settings holds the settings of syncing other settings of Windows like browsers, passwords, language and other preferences You can also select to sync the in-app purchases of apps and app which are purchased from Windows Store can also be synced so that you don't have to buy that app again in another PC.

## NOTE

This setting only syncs the settings from Internet Explorer and settings from other browsers won't be synced.

# App Data

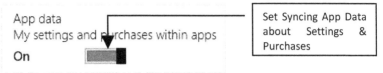

Figure 184: Syncing App Data

# Web Browser

Here you can select whether the settings like browser favorites, open tabs, home pages, history and settings are synced from this PC to cloud or not.

**NOTE**

Switches of All the Sync Settings in 'Other Settings' are Set to On by Default

# Passwords

This option lets you control whether the passwords from apps, websites, networks and home groups are synced to the cloud or not.

# Language Preferences

You would be able to control whether the keyboard settings, input methods, display language, personal dictionary and other language related settings are synced or not.

# Ease of Access

You can also choose to sync the ease of access settings like narrator, magnifier and more.

# Other Windows Settings

Other settings lets you select the File Explorer, mouse, pointers and other related settings are synced or not.

# Back Up Settings

Figure 185: Back Up Settings

If you want to back up your settings for this PC, turn the switch On.

# Metered Connections

Uploading the data from your PC to the SkyDrive on Metered Connections is important for the users. So, many settings are given in this section which displayed in Figure 165.

Figure 186: Using SkyDrive over Metered Connections

Following settings / switches are offered about the use of SkyDrive over Metered Connection:

1. Upload and download files over metered connections.
2. Upload and download files over metered connections even when you are roaming.

3. Sync and back up settings over metered connections.
4. Sync and back up settings over metered connections even when I'm roaming.

## NOTE

All switches about the upload and download of files on SkyDrive is On by Default.

**CHAPTER 9** »»

# Search, Search App, Share and Notifications

The search & apps page in the PC Settings holds all the options related to your apps, their behavior and other things.

Search & apps can also be used to see the app notification and the sizes of the apps as well.

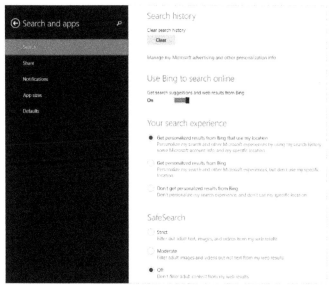

Figure 187: PC and Setting - Search and Apps

# Search

The search tab lets you control the search settings of the Windows 8.1 and its apps. Here you can also control the behavior of the deeply integrated Bing Search of Windows 8.1.

# Search History

This option does a simple job of clearing all search history of the Search options of Windows 8.1.

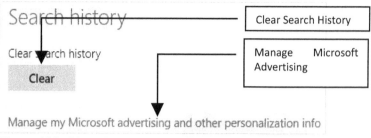
Figure 188: Clear Search History

Pressing 'Clear' button will clear all your history and things for which you searched and won't be kept in memory to show more relevant results in future.

Figure 189: Your Privacy and Microsoft Promotional Ads

About the management of Microsoft advertising and other personalization info, visit the Microsoft site (see Footnote 4).

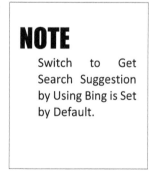

## NOTE

Switch to Get Search Suggestion by Using Bing is Set by Default.

# Use Bing to Search Online

Bing, the search engine by Microsoft, has been opted to work as the default search provider for the deep integrated search from Windows 8.1.

Windows 8.1 lets you control how the Bing effects (see the URL of the Microsoft Ads site[4]), your searches and how the results are showed.

Use Bing to search online — | Turn On the Switch to Use Bing for Search

Get search suggestions and web results from Bing

On

Figure 190: Switch to Use Bing for Search

# Your Search Experience

Here you can select how the search experience is customized for you, based on your location and other factors.

Your search experience

● Get personalized results from Bing that use my location
Personalize my search and other Microsoft experiences by using my search history, some Microsoft account info, and my specific location | This Radio Button is On by Default

○ Get personalized results from Bing
Personalize my search and other Microsoft experiences, but don't use my specific location

○ Don't get personalized results from Bing
Don't personalize my search experience, and don't use my specific location

Figure 191: Enhance Your Search Experience

Press any of the 3 radio buttons to search any of the following:

---

[4] http://choice.microsoft.com/en-us

# Get Personalized results from Bing that use my location

**NOTE**

'Get personalized results from Bing that use my Location' is Set by Default.

This options lets you choose whether the search results and suggestions are fetched from Bing or not using your internet connection and location.

# Get Personalized results from Bing

This option provides you the option to select whether the search results and suggestions are fetched from Bing.

# Don't get personalized results from Bing

This option is optimized not to get personalized results from Bing and not to use your location for the search purpose.

# Safe Search

If your PC is used by children and you want the search experience of Windows 8.1 to be safe for children and without any false language or results then, these safe search settings are best for you.

Figure 192: How to Conduct Safe Search

# Strict

This option lets you filter out any adult text, images and videos from search results whether they are from Bing or from your PC.

# Moderate

It lets you control and filter the adult images and videos from the search results but, the text isn't filtered.

# Off

It will completely turn off the adult filters and you would be showed adult images, videos and text results in the Search.

# Metered Connections

Figure 193: Getting Search on Metered Connections

Microsoft has also provided the option to let you select whether you want to sync the settings or not while using a metered connection so, that you don't end up using more than the provided data limit and you may have to pay extra.

# Sync and Back-up Settings over Metered Connections

This option lets you select the Windows sync settings while you are using a metered connection and roaming.

## Sync and backup settings over metered connection even when i'm roaming

**NOTE**

Search on Bing on Metered Connection is On by Default but Search while Roaming is Off.

This option can be used to stop the sync of settings while you are connected to a metered connection and roaming.

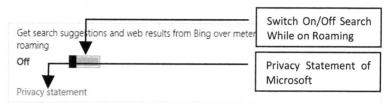

Switch On/Off Search While on Roaming

Privacy Statement of Microsoft

Figure 194: Get Suggestions from Web

# Privacy Statement

The Privacy Statement (see the link in Footnote[5]) takes you to the *'Windows 8.1 Preview and Windows Server 2012 R2 Preview privacy statement, Updated in June 2013'.*

---

[5]    http://windows.microsoft.com/en-US/windows-8/windows-8-1-privacy-statement?ocid=W8_UI#T1=highlights

Figure 195: Privacy Statement

# Share

Show apps I use most often at the top of the app list

On

Switch to Show Apps at Top which I Use Most

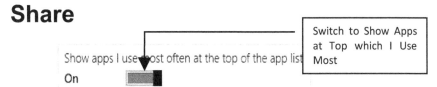

Figure 196: Frequent Used Apps at Top

The Share tab lets you control the sharing behavior or Windows 8.1 and the apps.

Figure 197: Search and Apps

You can select different options regarding sharing of apps using the Share Charm.

# Show Apps I Use Most Often at the Top of the App List

This option lets you select whether the apps which you use the most are showed on top of the sharing list or not.

# Show a List of How I Share Most Often

**NOTE**

Both the Switches to Show App at Top which I use and Share are On by Default.

Show a list of how I share most often

On

Switch to Show Apps at Top I Share Most

Figure 197: Display of Apps I Share Most

This option lets you select whether Windows suggests you the way of sharing depending on the previous sharing style or not.

# Items in list

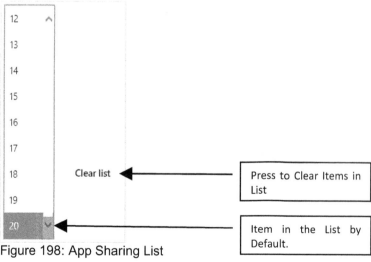

12
13
14
15
16
17
18

Clear list

19

20

Press to Clear Items in List

Item in the List by Default.

Figure 198: App Sharing List

This options lets you select how many apps are shown in the app sharing list. You can select up to 20 items.

# Use These App to Share

> **NOTE**
>
> There are 20 items in the list by Default.

This option lets you choose the apps which are showed in the sharing list of Windows 8.1 Share Charm. You can, manually, select whether an app is displayed in the list or not.

# Notification

This tab holds the options related to the notifications of Windows 8.1 and its apps. Here you can choose when notifications are shown, how they appear and which apps show notifications.

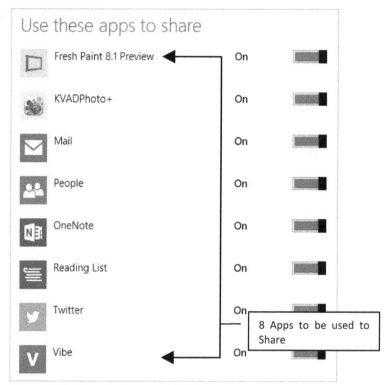

Figure 199: Apps to be used to Share

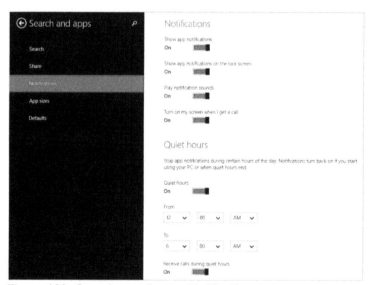

Figure 199: Search and Apps – Notifications

# Notifications

This section lets you control the general behavior of the apps like whether they appear or not and whether their sounds are played or not etc.

## Show App Notification

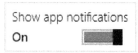

Figure 200: Switch to Show App Notifications

This switch is the main switch of all other notification related switches. You can choose whether the notifications are shown or not by moving the slider switch.

## Show App Notifications on the Lock Screen

Here you get the option to select whether the notifications are displayed on the lock screen or not.

Figure 201: Display of App Notification on Lock Screen

## Play Notification Sounds

Notifications in Windows 8.1 plays a specific sound when they appear. You can turn that sound Off, by using this switch.

Figure 202: Play of Notification Sounds

# Turning on My Screen Whenever I Get a Call

Figure 203: Turn on Screen When Get A Call

Here you get the options to choose whether your screen is turned on or not when you get a call from Skype or any other calling app.

## Quiet Hours

The quiet hours options in Windows 8.1 is relatively newer in this update for Windows 8. This cool options lets you select the hours on which you don't want to get the notifications.

If tuned on, you would be asked to select the timing in which you don't want to get the notifications from Windows. You can also select whether you can receive different calls during the selected period or not.

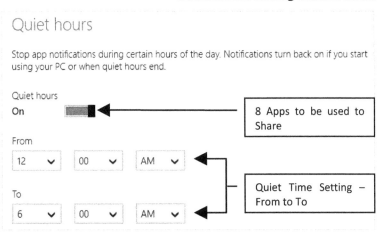

Figure 204: Setting of Quiet Hours

# Show Notifications from these Apps

This option lets you select the apps showing the notifications. You are provided a list of all the installed Modern-UI apps. There are many apps installed on your PC but you may select the important ones to give you notifications.

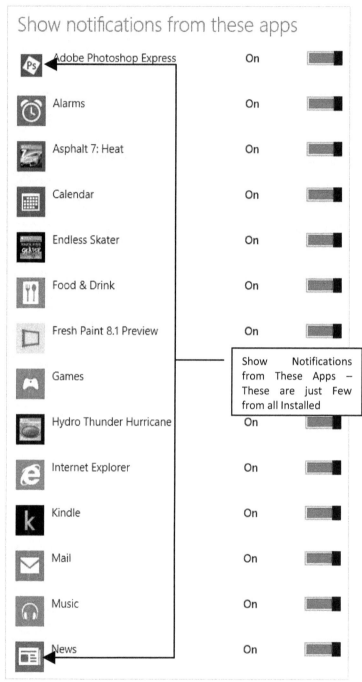

Figure 205: Show Notifications from These Apps

# App Sizes

In this window, Windows 8.1 offers you to see the sizes of all the apps installed. Windows 8.1 will tell you the space available for your apps and will give you the choice to either keep some apps or uninstall the apps which you do not deem to be important for your PC.

**NOTE**

Only Modern-UI apps are displayed in this list. Desktop x86 apps won't be showed in it.

Figure 206: App Sizes

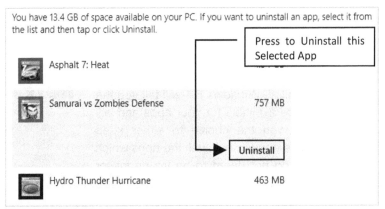

Figure 207: Uninstalling the Installed Apps

# Defaults - *Choose Default Apps*

At this window, you are given the choice to choose the default app from the given options. The defaults apps and their further choices are given below:

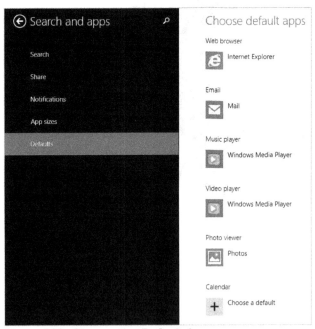

Figure 208: Choose the Default Apps

# Web Browser

Here you can select the default browser of your Windows 8. Internet Explorer is the default one but, you can choose other browsers like Firefox, Chrome and Opera etc. from the provided list.

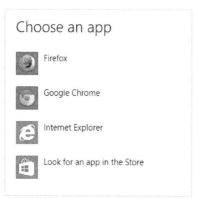

Figure 209: Select any App to use as the Web Browser as Default

# Email

This option lets you select the default app for sending and receiving emails. You can select from a couple of apps like Mail and Outlook etc.

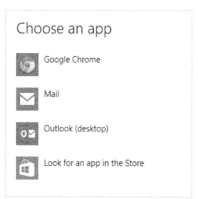

Figure 210: Choose an App to Use for Email as Default

# Music Player

Using this option, you can select the default music player app of Windows 8.1 which would be used to play all kinds of music on the PC as well.

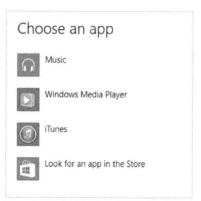

Figure 211: Choose an App for Music Playing as Default

# Video

You can also select the default video player app of Windows 8.1 using this option. The app you select would always be used to play all the videos on your PC.

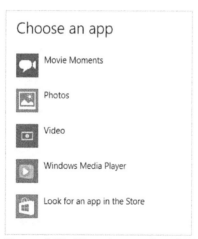

Figure 212: Choosing an App for Videos Playing as Default

# Photo Viewer

The default photo viewer app of Windows 8.1 can be selected from this option. It would be used to open all the photos on this PC.

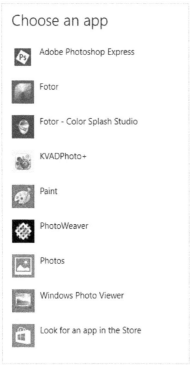

Figure 213: Choosing an App for Photo Viewing as Default

# Calendar

This option lets you select the default calendar app of Windows 8.1 which can be used to open up calendar tasks.

## NOTE

This option doesn't have any default instead, you are given the option to select the app from Store.

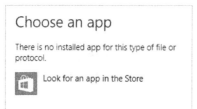

Figure 214: Choosing an App for Calendar Use as Default

# Maps App

Anything related to maps and locations would be opened in the app, you select, using this option.

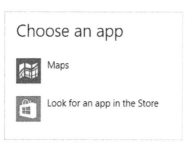

Figure 215: Choosing Map App as Default

**NOTE**

You may select any app, other than given above. You may select any app from the Store and may select it as the default one.

# Default Apps by File Type

Pressing this option will take you to a large selection of file, named as; Associate File Types with Specific Apps, from where you may select any of the default app from the list of hundreds of default apps and associate with your desired file types.

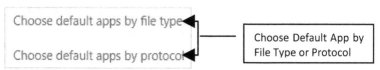

Figure 216: Choosing Default Apps by File Type or By Protocol

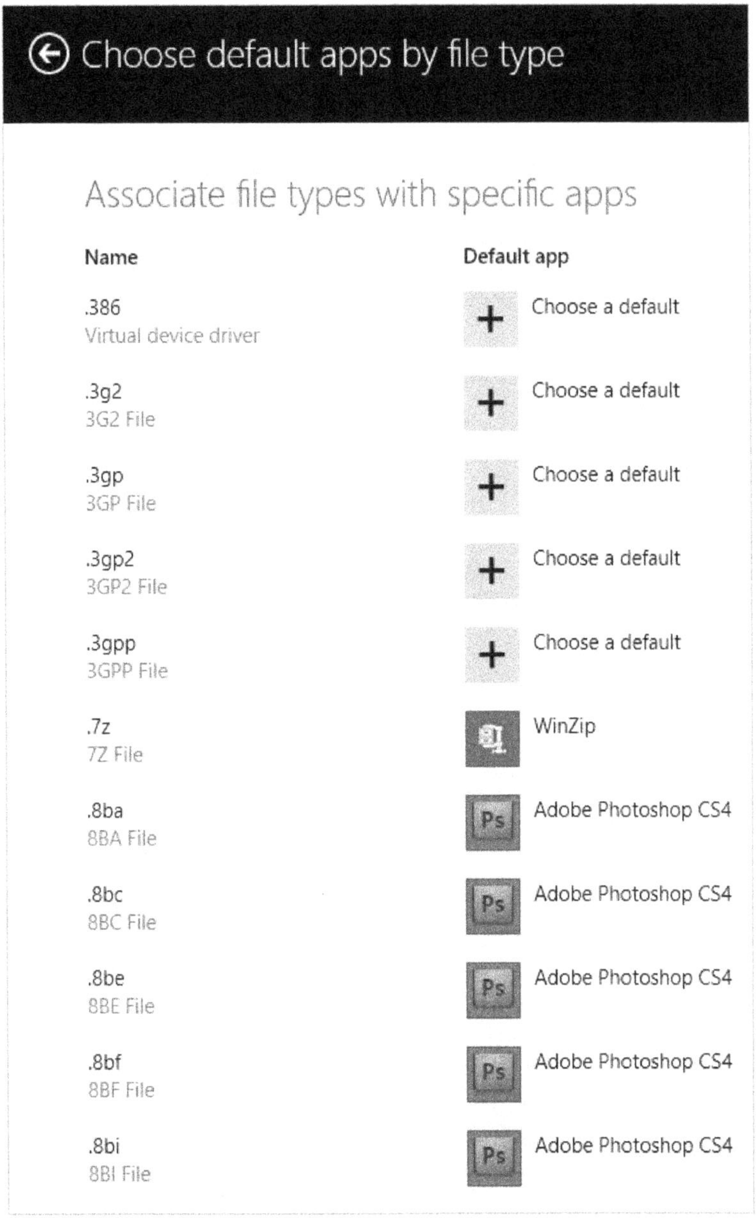

⊖ Choose default apps by file type

Associate file types with specific apps

| Name | Default app |
|------|-------------|
| .386<br>Virtual device driver | ➕ Choose a default |
| .3g2<br>3G2 File | ➕ Choose a default |
| .3gp<br>3GP File | ➕ Choose a default |
| .3gp2<br>3GP2 File | ➕ Choose a default |
| .3gpp<br>3GPP File | ➕ Choose a default |
| .7z<br>7Z File | 🗜 WinZip |
| .8ba<br>8BA File | Ps Adobe Photoshop CS4 |
| .8bc<br>8BC File | Ps Adobe Photoshop CS4 |
| .8be<br>8BE File | Ps Adobe Photoshop CS4 |
| .8bf<br>8BF File | Ps Adobe Photoshop CS4 |
| .8bi<br>8BI File | Ps Adobe Photoshop CS4 |

Figure 217: Choosing Default Apps by File Type

# Default Protocols with Specific Apps

At this window, you will be given options to select any specific apps, from various protocols, depending upon your need.

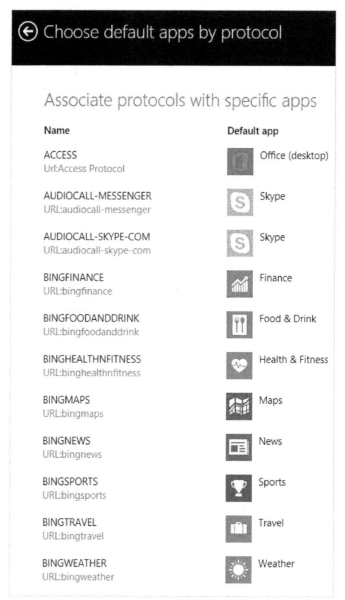

Figure 218: Associate Protocol with Specific Apps

**CHAPTER 10**

# Privacy

# PC Settings - Privacy

Privacy page in the PC Setting holds all the options related to your privacy in different situations like search and apps etc.

**NOTE**

You also get the option to turn on/off these options during installation of Windows 8.1.

Figure 219: Privacy Options

Let's have a look upon each of the 5 settings.

# General

General tab of PC Settings holds the options like the permission which the Windows 8.1 has to your private items like account picture, you name and other sensitive information.

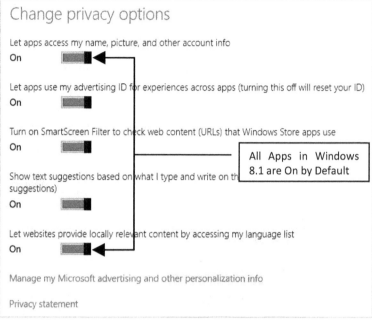

Figure 220: Changing Privacy Settings

# Let Apps Access my Name, Picture and Other Account Info

Windows 8.1, by default, gives the permissions to apps to access your name, picture and other information from your account to display the things for user friendly but, you can disable that access by switching off this slider switch.

# Turn on Smart Screen Filter to Check Web Content (URLs) that Windows Store Apps Use

This options lets you keep your PC secure from malware and other things which may compromise the security of your PC and may result in the hacking, as well. Smart Screen Filter can be turned 'On' to scan each and every link you open in your Windows 8.1 to keep your PC safe.

# Show Text Suggestions Based on What I Type and Write on this PC

This option lets you turn off the text suggestions which you get while typing different things in the Windows like web addresses, named and other things.

## NOTE

Turning this option Off will also turn off the ability to control individual app access to your location.

# Let Websites Provide Locally Relevant Content by Accessing My Language List

This option is best for people who use search of Windows 8.1 a lot and remain always connected to the Internet. This options lets the Windows provide relevant content depending on your language preferences.

One more option about the Microsoft advertisement privacy preferences leads to the Microsoft page about the personalized ads upon the advertisements on the pages, frequently visited by you.[6]

The other option about the privacy statement would take you to the Windows 8.1 and Windows Servers 2012 R2 Privacy Statement, mentioned upon the web site given in the foot note.[7]

# Location

Location tab in the PC Settings lets you control the location preferences of your PC. You can select whether apps and Windows can access your location and which app use your location.

## NOTE

All the 5 switch options are On by Default.

---

[6]http://choice.microsoft.com/en-us
[7]http://windows.microsoft.com/en-US/windows-8/windows-8-1-privacy-statement?ocid=W8_UI#T1=highlights.

# Windows and Apps Use My Location

This options lets you turn On or Off the location access by Windows.

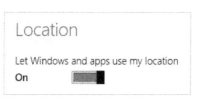

Figure 221: Allowing Windows to Use your Location

**NOTE**

Switches of all the Apps in this section is On by Default.

# Let these apps use my location

This option provides you a list of apps which can access your location. Here you have the choice to select which app can access your location and which can't by turning the slider switch On and Off.

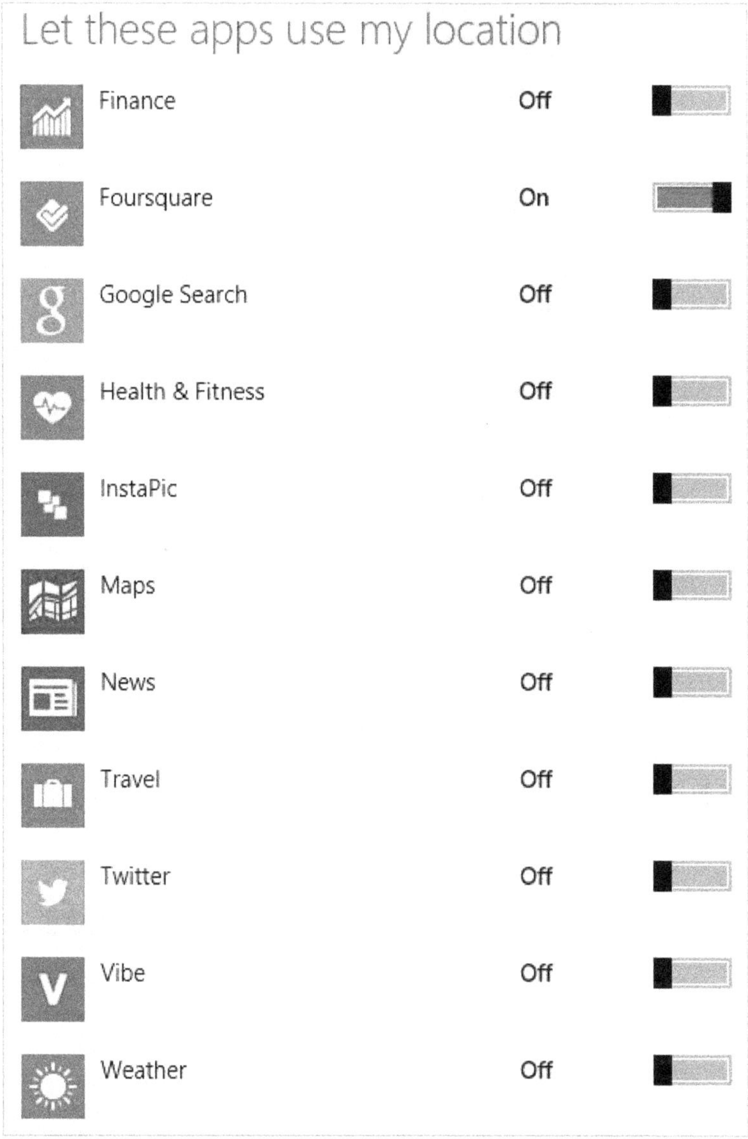

## Let these apps use my location

| | | |
|---|---|---|
| Finance | Off | |
| Foursquare | On | |
| Google Search | Off | |
| Health & Fitness | Off | |
| InstaPic | Off | |
| Maps | Off | |
| News | Off | |
| Travel | Off | |
| Twitter | Off | |
| Vibe | Off | |
| Weather | Off | |

Figure 222: Allowing the Apps to Use Location of Your PC

# Webcam

Webcam option in the PC Settings lets you control the webcam related settings of Windows 8.1. For example, which apps can access the webcam and which apps use your webcam etc.

Figure 223: Web Cam Settings

# Let Apps Use My Webcam

This switch is the master switch for all the webcam accesses by apps in your Windows 8.1. Turn this On if you want to give the permission or turn it Off if you don't want the apps to access your webcam.

# Let These Apps Use My Webcam

This options provides a list of all the apps installed on your PC, which can access your webcam. Here you can grant the permission by moving slider switch to On position against each app.

## NOTE

Turning the master switch Off will also disable the capability to select individual apps which can access your webcam.

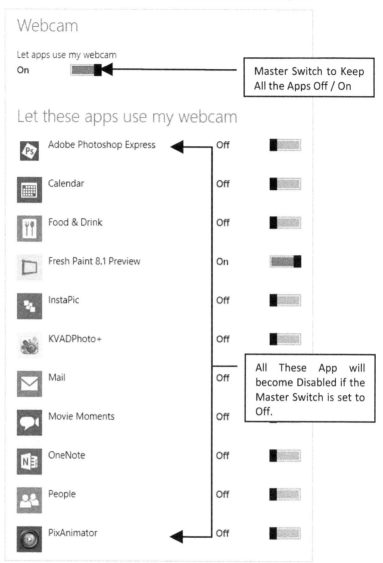

Figure 224: Using the Apps for the Web Cam

# Microphone

Microphone page in PC Settings holds the options regarding your microphone. Here you can control whether apps and Windows 8.1 can use your microphone or not and individual app access to microphone can also be controlled.

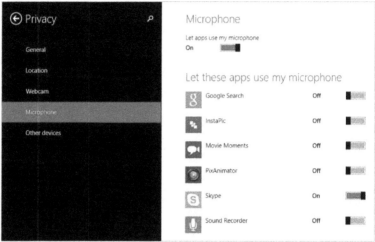

Figure 225: Setting of Apps for Microphone

# Let Apps Use My Microphone

This options is the master switch to control the access to your microphone by apps. Turn this On if you want to give permissions to apps to use your microphone.

**NOTE**

Turning the master switch Off which also disable the capability to switch off the individual app access to microphone.

# Let These Apps Use My Microphone

Here you can control which apps use your microphone. You can turn off the slider switch against each app to stop the app from using your microphone.

**NOTE**

All the Apps in this section are not allowed to use Microphone by Default.

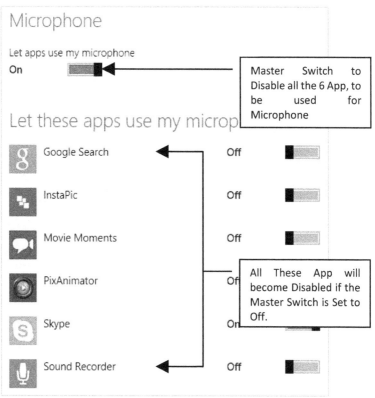

Figure 226: Setting Apps for the Microphone

# Other Devices

This tab will show all the other apps which may access your private information. But, other than the above things, there are hardly any device which may require access to your private information.

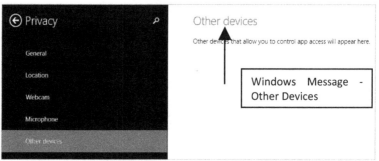

Figure 227: Other Devices

**CHAPTER 11**

# Networks

Network page in the PC Settings is the one place settings for all your network related configurations. Here, you can check network status of your PC, add VPN, configure radio devices, set proxy settings, connect to home group and workplace.

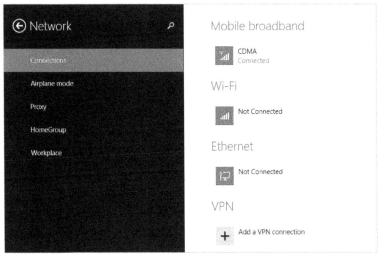

Figure 228: Networks

# Connections

Connection tab in the PC Settings lets you connect and see all the available network connections.

# Mobile Broadband

Here all the mobile broadband connection would be displayed which are available and connected, if any. In our case, it was CDMA.

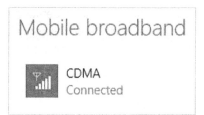

Figure 229: Status of Mobile Broadband

Pressing CDMA, will give you instructions to share this connection.

# Wi-Fi

Wi-Fi section lets you discover and connect to your Wi-Fi connections. You can also press any Wi-Fi connection to get its details like encryption, strength and IP address etc.

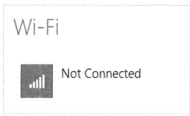

Figure 230: Status of Wi-Fi

# Ethernet

Ethernet connections also known as LAN networks can be seen here. If you are connected to Ethernet connection, pressing would take you to its details page where info about driver, network status and IP address etc. are displayed.

Figure 231: Ethernet not Connected

# VPN

Windows 8.1 also supports VPN connection configuration without the need to install any third party app. Simply, press the 'Add a VPN connection' and a pop-up will open asking for details about the VPN network.

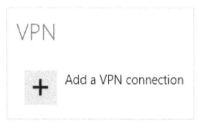

Figure 232: Adding a VPN Connection

Figure 233: Add a Network Connection

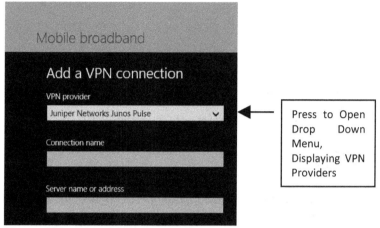

Figure 234: Add a VPN Connection

If you add Microsoft in the drop down menu, you will be asked to provide additional info like given in the image below.

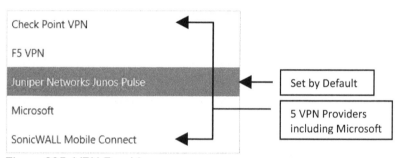

Figure 235: VPN Providers

Now, you will be asked to give additional info.

Figure 236: Add a VPN Connection
In the drop down menu of Type of Sign-in-info, you would be required to select one of the options:
1.  Username or Password
2.  Smartcard

210

3. One Time Password

After adding the required info, the due process will be completed, according to set process.

# Airplane Mode

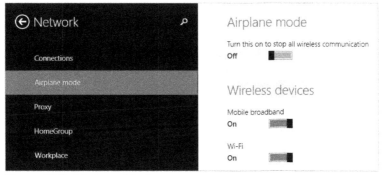

Figure 237: Airplane Mode

When the Airplane mode switch is turned On, all communications will be disabled.

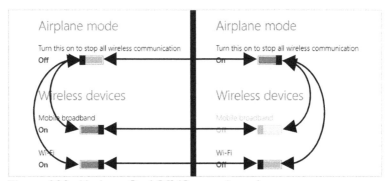

Figure 238: Airplane On / Off (Comparisons)

As soon as you will turn the master switch On, both the Mobile Broadband and Wi-Wi will be disabled.

# Proxy

Proxy tab in PC Settings lets you control the proxy configuration of your PC. You can turn On / Off proxy and configure the proxy settings.

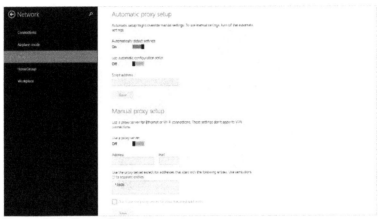

Figure 239: Proxy Settings

# Automatic Proxy Setup

Windows 8.1 also comes with built-in proxy settings where you just have to insert the configuration values and the proxy starts functioning.

Figure 240: Automatic Proxy Setup

## NOTE

To make the automatic configuration script working, you will have to provide the exact path of the script to make the proxy working automatically.

# Automatic Detect Setting

As the automatic proxy setup may cause to override manual setting, done by you, you are required to turn off the automatic settings by switch On or Off the automatic detect setting.

# Use Automatic Configuration Script

One more option is to use the automatic configuration script by switching On or Off. If you set the Switch On, you will have to give the Script Address and then save it.

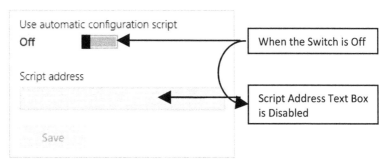

Figure 241: Using Automatic Configuration Script

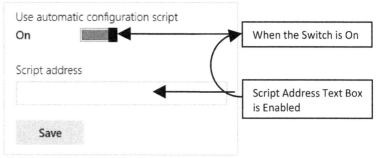

Figure 242: Using Automatic Configuration Script

# Manual Proxy Setup

If you prefer to use manual proxy settings with each and every setting configured by you then, this option is best for you.

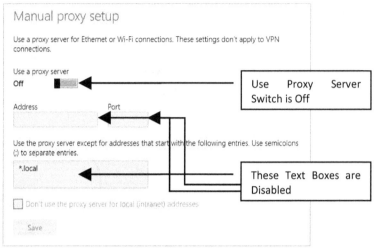

Figure 243: Manual Proxy Server

If you want to use a proxy server with your custom configuration, turn on the option from slider switch and add the appropriate options in the address and port boxes.

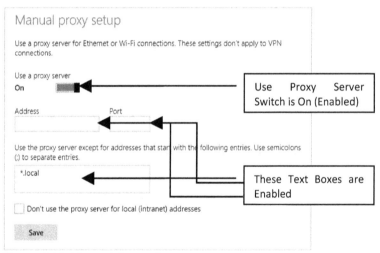

Figure 244: Manual Proxy Setup

You can also add the address on which you don't want to use the proxy settings.

# Home Group

Figure 245: Home Group

Home Group section of desktop Control Panel has been moved to the Modern-UI PC Settings but, its overall working is still the same. As this Section is included in the Control Panel of the Windows, it is not specifically covered in this book.

# Workplace

Pressing the Workplace option will take you to the window of Workplace. If you are willing to get access to your workplace or turn on your device management, enter your user ID here in the place given for the purpose and click join.

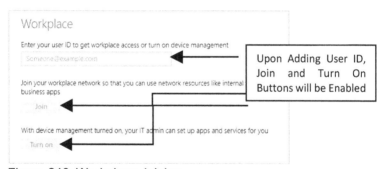

Figure 246: Workplace Joining

And if you are willing to allow apps and services from IT admin, press Turn On button, given at the lower end of the Workplace window.

215

**CHAPTER 12**

# Setting Time & Languages

# Time and Language

Figure 247: Time and Luggage

# Date and Time - Set Time Automatically

If you want the Windows to set the time of your PC automatically depending on the internet time, turn On this option.

**NOTE**

If you prefer to set your own time and always make adjustments to your PC time, by yourself, don't turn this option on or Windows will continuously correct the time when you make changes.

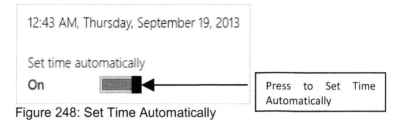

Figure 248: Set Time Automatically

# Change Date and Time

You can also change the date and time of your PC from here. Pressing the Change button will open up a pop-up menu where you can select the time and date.

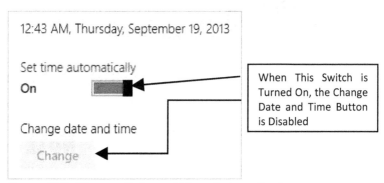

Figure 249: Change Date and Time Automatically

Upon turning the 'Set Time Automatically, On, the change Date and Time button is enabled. When it is pressed, the new popup will appear, giving you option to set date and time as per your need.

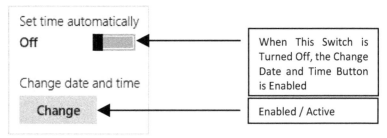

Figure 250: Change Date and Time

Upon pressing the Change button will open up a popup where you will be given option to set the time and date as per your desire.

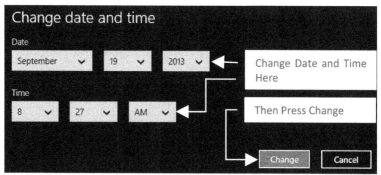

Figure 251: Change ate and Time

# Time Zone

Time Zone of your PC can also be changed from here. Simply select your desired time zone from the drop down list and your time zone would be changed.

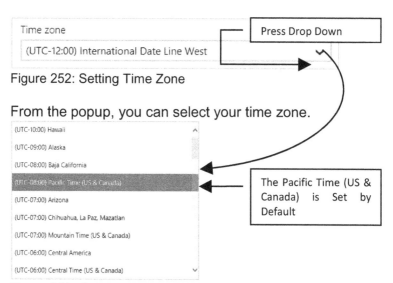

Figure 252: Setting Time Zone

From the popup, you can select your time zone.

Figure 253: Choose Your Time Zone

# Adjusting for Daylight Saving Time Automatically

If you want to use the daylight saving time option then, you may enable the option by turning the slider switch to 'On'.

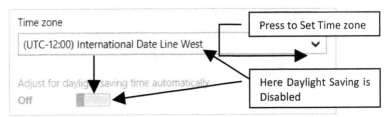

Figure 254: Daylight Saving is Disabled at Date Line

For the International Date Line West Time Zone, the option to adjust the daylight saving time will be disabled. But, you if you select, e.g. Alaska Time, this option would be enabled for you to switch On or Off accordingly to your need.

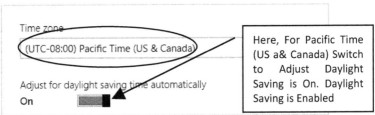

Figure 255: Adjusting Daylight Saving Time Automatically for International Date Line

# Date and Time Format

This option shows date and time formats of your PC where you are shown first day of week, short date, long date, short & long time etc.

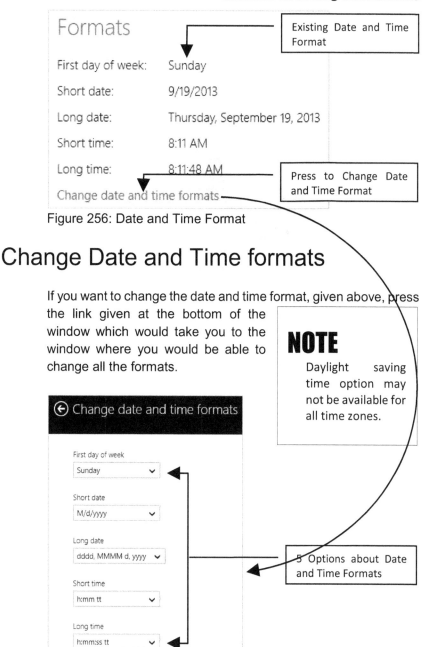

Figure 256: Date and Time Format

# Change Date and Time formats

If you want to change the date and time format, given above, press the link given at the bottom of the window which would take you to the window where you would be able to change all the formats.

**NOTE**

Daylight saving time option may not be available for all time zones.

Figure 257: Change Date and Time Formats

# Region and Language

This tab performs two different yet important tasks i.e. country or region and languages selection.

Figure 258: Time and Language

# Country or Region

Here you would be provided a drop down menu to select out of 268 given countries or regions – starting from Afghanistan to Zimbabwe – to be used to give local content based on you location.

**NOTE**

United States is Set as Default.

Figure 259: Setting Country and Region

Upon pressing the drop down menu, you will be offered a list of the countries to select from.

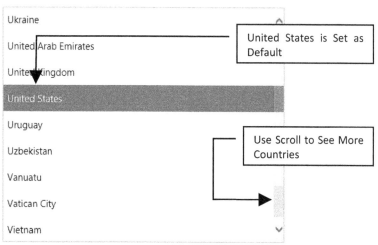

Figure 260: Changing Country & Region

# Languages

**NOTE**

If you want to add a specific language, you would need a keyboard to be added to enable you to write in that language. Pressing 'Add a language' would open up a window where 139 different languages are displayed for you to select from.

The available languages and settings up the default language may differ from Windows 8.1 version depending on language pack you are using.

You can also configure an installed language by pressing it and selecting 'Options' where options like hand writing style, and keyboard language can be selected.

Figure261:Adding a Language

You can also remove or make some other language the primary one by using the Remove and Set as primary buttons.

# Add a Language – Language Options

To add a language, press this button to open a new window.

Figure 262: Adding a Language

Options for Setting Primary Language: As the English (United States) is set as default, you would be offered to select from the options, such as, pressing the Windows Display Language, the resulting popup will offer the Option to explore further options Upon Language Options (*Hand Writing*):

Figure 263: Hand Writing Options

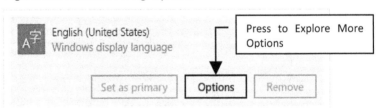

Figure 264: Windows Language Display Options for US

# Language Options (*Hand Writing*)

This drop down menu will offer two further options:

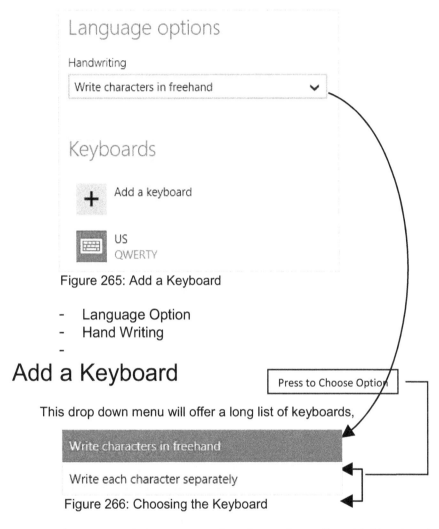

Figure 265: Add a Keyboard

- Language Option
- Hand Writing
-

# Add a Keyboard

Press to Choose Option

This drop down menu will offer a long list of keyboards,

Figure 266: Choosing the Keyboard

Qwerty and Azerty, starting from Canadian Multinational Qwerty and ending at Yoruba Qwerty. It is up to you to select the most appropriate one for your PC.

1. Keyboard Options

2. Add a Keyboard
3. US Qwerty

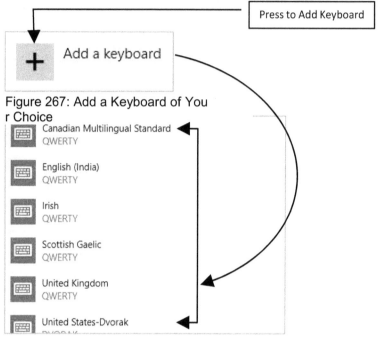

Figure 267: Add a Keyboard of Your Choice

Figure 268: List of Keyboards Available

Alternatively, you will be asked to remove the US Qwerty which is set by default.

**CHAPTER 13** »»

# Ease of Access

Ease of Access page of PC Settings holds all the options like narrator, magnifier, High contrast, keyboard, and more. All the things can be configured and their default behavior can also be changed.

Figure 269: Ease of Access

# Narrator

Windows 8.1, just like Windows 8, includes a narrator which lets you narrate what you see on your screen. All the settings which, previously, could be found on desktop Control Panel have been moved to the PC Settings which is pretty much the same in working.

Hear what's on the screen

Figure 270: Hear Text and Controls on Screen

The first thing you would need to do is to Switch On the Narrator. Immediately after switching On of the Narrator, a speaker would start, automatically, telling you about each function of Windows 8.1 which is being performed by you on your PC.

# Start Narrator Automatically

If you want the narrator to start narrating the things on the screen automatically, you may enable this option.

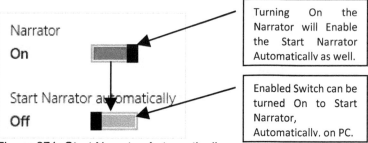

Figure 271: Start Narrator Automatically

Turning the switch 'Narrator' On will enable whole the setting on the Narrator windows. Now, you may turn On the 'Start Narrator Automatically'.

# Voice

Upon switching the Narrator On, the Voice option would be enabled where you may see the following settings displayed in image:

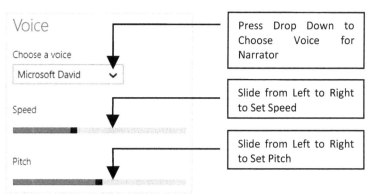

Figure 272: Choose Voice, Its Speed and Pitch

# Choose a Voice

You can also change the narrator voice which would let you customize the vocals of the narrations.

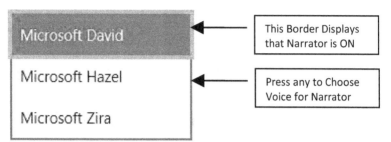

Figure 273: Choose the Voice for Narrator

You can select the voice from options like Microsoft David, Microsoft Hazel and Microsoft Zira.

# Speed

You can also customize the speed of narration. Moving the slider from left to right increase the narration speed.

# Pitch

If you don't like the pitch of the sound you are hearing from narrator, you can use the given slider to adjust the pitch of sound.

# **Sounds You Hear**
# Read Hints for Controls and Buttons

This option lets you control whether the narrator read the hints for controls and buttons or not.

# Characters you Type

You can also choose if the characters you type using the keyboard are spoken by narrator or not.

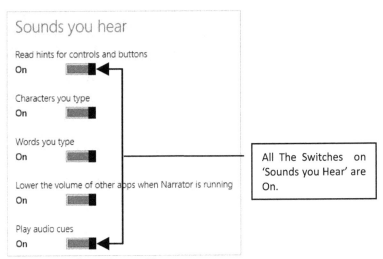

Figure 274: Sounds you Hear

# Words you Type

You also have the option to select whether the words you type are narrated by narrator or not.

## NOTE

All the Switches About the sounds you Hear are On by Default.

# Lower the Volume of Other Apps When App is Running

If you turn On the narrator and use other device who produce sound, hearing the narrator might be difficult. You can use this option to reduce the volume of other apps if, narrator is running.

# Play Audio Clues

Here you have the option to select whether the audio tips from different buttons and menu are narrated by narrator or not.

## Cursors and Keys

Here you will see the following options:

1. Highlight the Cursor
2. Insertion Point Follow the Narrator
3. Activation of Touch Keyboard whenever I Lift my Fingers off the Keyboard.

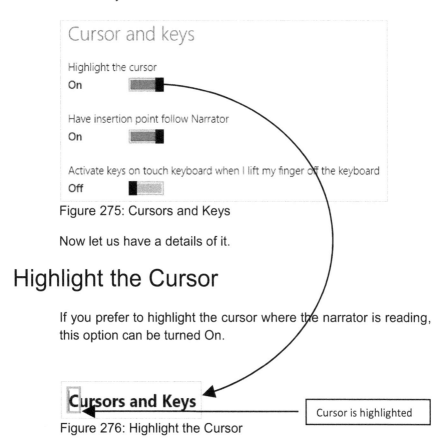

Figure 275: Cursors and Keys

Now let us have a details of it.

# Highlight the Cursor

If you prefer to highlight the cursor where the narrator is reading, this option can be turned On.

Figure 276: Highlight the Cursor

# Insertion Point Follow the Narrator

If you want the cursor to be at the place which is being narrated, you may enable this option. Enabling it would give you the ability to start insertion characters or text where the narrator is reading.

Figure 277: Insertion Point to follow Narrator

# Activation of Touch Keyboard whenever I would lift my Fingers from the Keyboard

If you want the touch keyboard (*if available*) to be enabled when you holds the fingers of the touch screen, you can enable this option by using slider switch.

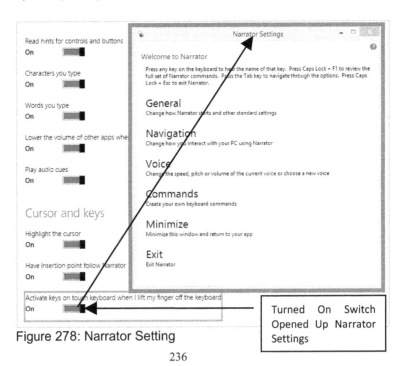

Figure 278: Narrator Setting

After turning On the 'Activate Keys on Touch Keyboard when I lift my fingers off the keyboard', the popup setting will appear on the desktop.

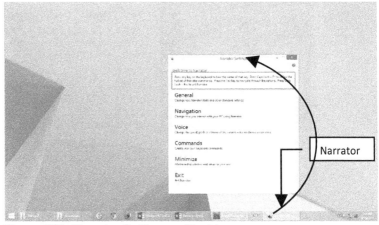

Figure 279: Narrator Setting on Desktop

# Magnifier

This option was available in previous Windows versions as well, but in Windows 8.1 this option is significantly improved. The purpose of this option is to facilitate users with long sightedness, i.e. those who feel problems to read computer screen due to their eye sight.

# Magnify Things on the Screen

Here, you will be given options to run magnifier.

Figure 280: Magnifying Things on the Screen

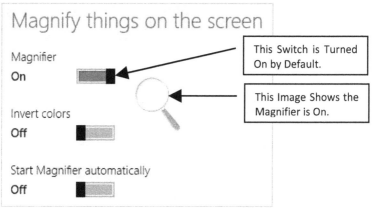

Figure 281: Magnify Things on Screen

If you want to enable the magnifier, turn it on by using the slider switch.

As soon as the Magnifier switch is turned On, the magnifier appears on screen with default options enabled.

# Plus / Minus Options

In the magnifier, one '+' and one '-' buttons are available to magnify the screen up to 1600% or the screen size can be minimized accordingly.

# View

You can also select the view which are used by magnifier.

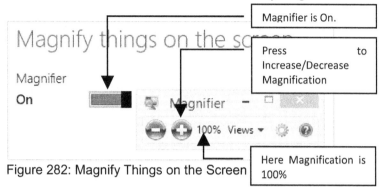

Figure 282: Magnify Things on the Screen

# Full Screen

This option, if selected, would enlarge whole the screen area, as per selected option.

**NOTE**

All these four switch options are disabled by default. When the Magnifier switch is turned On, all these 4 options are enabled but will be Off by default.

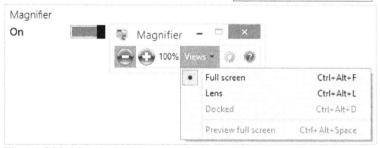

Figure 283: Viewer in the Magnifier

# Lens

This option will provide you with a rectangle magnifying glass like tool, which can be used exactly like a magnifying glass.

# Docked

This option will provide a larger area, magnified.

# Preview Full Screen

This option will provide a much wider area, magnified, and whenever any object is highlighted, it would further enlarge it by focusing on it.

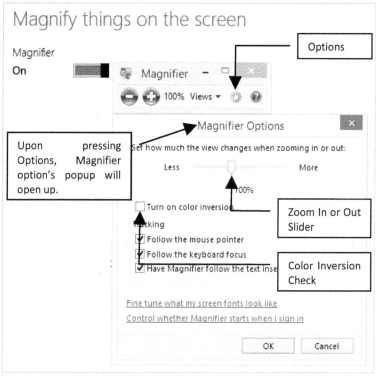

Figure 284: Magnify Things on Screen

# Invert Colors

When this option is checked, all the colors of the screen will be inverted. This option is, perhaps, included in the Windows 8.1 with a purpose to help those people who have color blindness to some of the colors.

Figure 285: Color is inverted.

# Start Magnifier Automatically

This option lets you select whether the Magnifier is started automatically under certain circumstances or not. If the Magnifier switch is turned On, 'Start Magnifier Automatically' is enabled and can be turned on automatically.

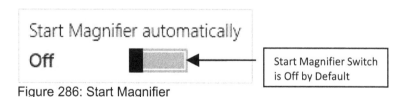

Figure 286: Start Magnifier

# Tracking

Tracking options are also attached with the magnifier switch. As soon as the magnifier switch is turned On, the Tracking would also be enabled.

# Follow the Keyboard Focus

If you want the magnifier to follow the keyboard, turn this option on. Turning it on would make the magnifier follow the keyboard inputs.

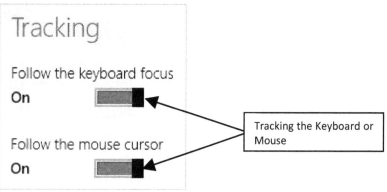

Figure 287: Tracking Options

# Follow the Mouse Cursor

You can also choose to let the magnifier follow the mouse cursor so that the location where the mouse cursor is taken, gets zoomed up.

# High Contrast – Choose a Theme

High Contrast tab of PC Settings lets you select and customize the high contrast themes of Windo/ws 8.1.

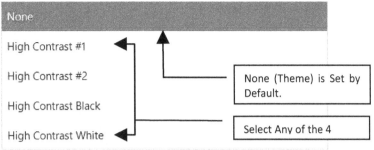

Figure 288: Theme Options

# Choose a theme

You are provided a total of 4 different high contrast themes, i.e. High Contrast#1, High Contrast #2, High Contrast Black and High Contrast White to select from.

# Theme High Contrast # 1

Figure 289: High Contrast Theme # 1

From each theme, you will be asked to select colors of:

➤ Text
➤ Hyperlinks
➤ Disabled Text
➤ Selected Text

243

> ➢ Button Text
> ➢ Background Color

Figure 290: High Contrast White

After selecting the appropriate setting, press apply and the display of the Windows will be almost fascinating, as per your settings.

# Keyboard

Windows 8.1, just like the Windows 8, includes an on-screen keyboard but, the settings could be found in desktop Control Panel. Now, the settings have been moved to the PC Settings where the options are same.

Figure 291: On Screen Keyboard

# On-Screen Keyboard

This option lets you turn On or Off the on-screen keyboard which will also toggle the other switches.

The On-Screen Keyboard is Off by Default.

Figure 292: On Screen Keyboard

When you will turn the On-Screen Keyboard switch to On, the On-Screen keyboard will appear on the screen of your PC.

On-Screen Keyboard Toggle Switch is On and the On-Screen Key Board is Available.

Figure 293: On-Screen Keyboard

# Useful Keys

Following options will be displayed about the Useful Keys:

- ➢ Sticky Keys
- ➢ Toggle Keys
- ➢ Filter Keys

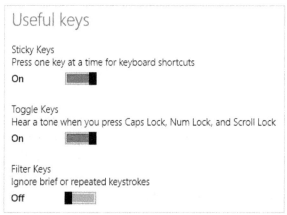
Figure 294: Useful Keys

# Sticky Keys

This option lets you choose whether the keyboard shortcuts from on-screen keyboard required pressing of one key at a time or all keys at a time or not.

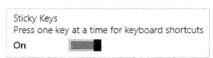
Figure 295: Sticky Keyboards Shortcuts

Pressing it would require only one key press using on-screen keyboard.

# Toggle Keys

If you want to get notified when the Caps Lock, NumLock and Scroll Lock are enabled then, enable this option.

Figure 296: Toggle Keys

You would be notified with a tone when you start typing and any of these three keys are enabled.

# Filter Keys

You can also select to filter out same key strokes if any key is pressed repeatedly.

Figure 297: Filter Keys

# Mouse

Mouse options page in the PC Settings lets you control the mouse related settings like pointer size, pointer color and mouse cursor behavior.

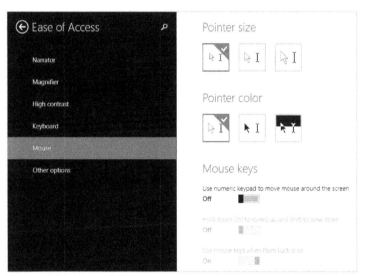

Figure 298: Mouse Settings

Following Mouse options are offered at this window:

# Pointer Size

Here you can select the pointer size from a total of 3 different sizes.

Pressing any size would change the pointer size to that.

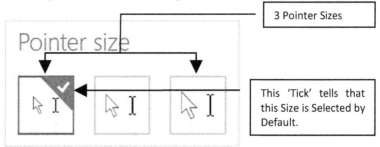

Figure 299: Pointer Size

# Point Color

You can also select the color of your pointer for three different options i.e. white, black and black & white.

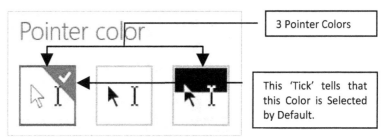

Figure 300: Pointer Color

# Mouse Keys

This section lets you control the behavior of mouse cursor when you are using the numeric keys on the physical keyboard.

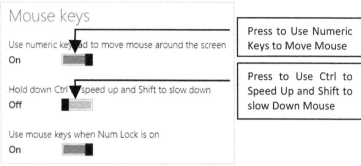

Figure 301: Mouse Keys

# Use Numeric Keypad to Move Mouse Around the Screen

This options lets you control whether the mouse cursor can be moved with the numeric keypad of the physical keyboard or not.

# Hold Down Ctrl to Speed Up and Shift to Slow Down

This options, if enabled, will let you speed up the cursor movements while using the numeric keypad to navigate.

# Use mouse keys when NumLock is turned on

This options lets you choose whether the mouse keys can be used while the NumLock is turned on in the keyboard.

# Other Options – Visual Options

Other options page of the PC Settings lets you control some other settings of Windows like animations, windows backgrounds and the notification display time etc.

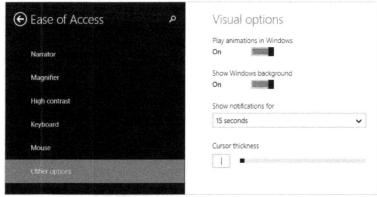
Figure 302: Visual Options

# *More Options*
# Play Animation in Windows

This options lets you enable or disable the Windows 8.1 Modern-UI animations which are displayed while performing different operations.

Turning this option Off will disable all animations and Windows 8.1 won't use any transitions while performing tasks.

Figure 303: Play Animations in Windows

# Show Windows Background

This option lets you select whether the Start Screen and desktop backgrounds are shown or not. Turning it off will disable all backgrounds.

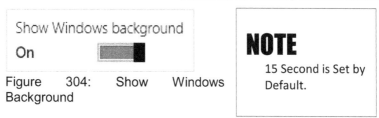

Figure 304: Show Windows Background

# Show Notifications For

This option lets you select the notification display time, i.e. for how long the notifications are displayed.

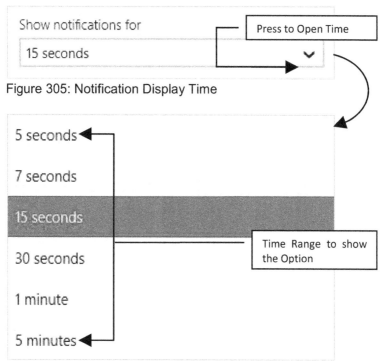

Figure 305: Notification Display Time

Figure 306: Show of Notification Time

You can select from different options like:

- 5 seconds
- 7 seconds
- 15 seconds
- 30 seconds

251

- 1 minute
- 5 minutes

# Cursor Thickness

If you like the mouse cursor of Windows PC to be thicker than normal, this options is best for you. Move slider from left to right to increase the cursor thickness. See the difference before and after opting for the thick cursor.

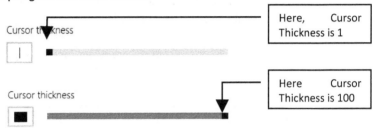

**CHAPTER 14**

# Windows Updates & Recovery

*Saadat Wahid, Muzzammil Waheed and Ahmad Wahid*

In this section of Windows, you are shown all the available updates which are ready to be installed on your PC.

# Update and Recovery

This page in the PC Settings holds all the options related to Windows Updates, Windows recovery and file history features.

## NOTE

You can also view the details of each update by pressing the Detailed link against each available update.

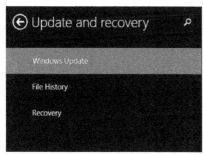

Figure 307: Windows Update and Recovery

# Windows Update

This feature lets you control the behavior of Windows Updates, how they are installed and which updates are installed.

# View Details

Pressing this link will take you to another details page where the available updates and their details are showed. Here you can select individual updates to install and the updates are also sorted in different categories like 'Important and Recommended' etc.

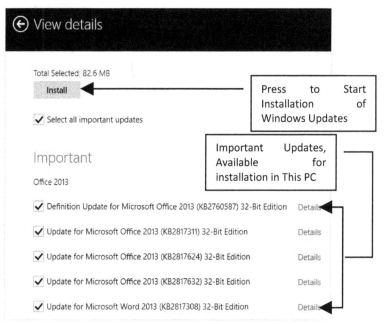

Figure 308: View Details

# View Your Update History

This option lets you see the history of updates. You can see which updated were installed on your PC and whether they were successfully installed or some error occurred.

# Choose How Updates Get Installed

Pressing this link will take you to the configuration page of Windows Updates where you can choose how and when the updated are installed.

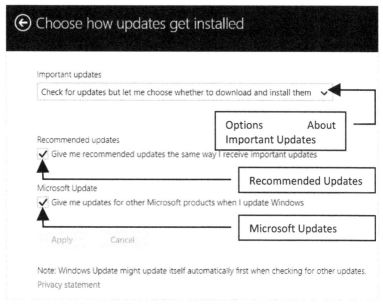

Figure 309: Choose How Updates Get Installed

You are also provided the option to receive the recommended updates, provided to you, in the same way as important updates. The option to get updated for different Microsoft products is also there.

# Check for the Updates But Let Me Choose Whether to Download and Install

Here you will be offered 4 different options, such as:

➢ Install updates automatically (*recommended*).
➢ Download updates but let me choose whether to install them or not.

**NOTE**

'Check for Updates but let me choose whether to download and install them' is Set by Default.

257

➢ Check for updates but let me choose whether to download and install them or not.

➢ Never check for updates (*not reco*

Figure 310: Important Updates Installations

# File History

File history is the feature first introduced in Windows 8. This awesome feature, if enabled, will take backup of your selected files on the device you opted. The backups can be configured, automatically, on daily or periodic basis.

Figure 311: Saves Copies of Files Automatically

# File History

This option lets you turn On or Off the file history feature. If enabled, you would also be able to configure the files which are backed up and the device on which the files are backed up.

# Select a Drive

Pressing the Select a drive link will open up a pop up menu where you can select the appropriate device to back up your files.

# Backup Now

If you have enabled the file history feature and selected the backup drive, you may press the 'Back up now' button to back up all your file to the device right now.

# **Recovery**

Windows 8 was the first operating system by Microsoft which included advanced backup features. In Windows 8.1, you can now refresh your PC without losing files, apps and settings or you may 'factory reset' your PC easily without much haste. You can also select the advanced startup option from this tab where advanced options like safe mode, boot from device etc. can be accessed.

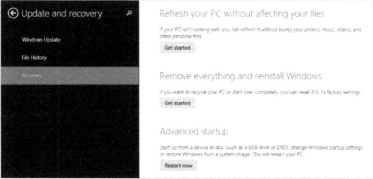

Figure 312: Refreshing your PC without Affecting Your Files

# Refresh Your PC without Affecting Your Files

This option lets you refresh the Windows installation without affecting your files, apps and personalization.

If your Windows 8.1 PC isn't functioning properly, you may use this feature to refresh Windows installation.

Refresh your PC without affecting your files

If your PC isn't running well, you can refresh it without losing your photos, music, videos, and other personal files.

Get started

Figure 312: Installing Windows with Back up of All Files

# Remove Everything and Reinstall Windows

If you are selling your Windows 8.1 PC to someone else and want to erase each and everything thing from the PC, then you can reset the PC to its factory settings.

**NOTE**

You will need a Windows installation media like a DVD or ISO file to proceed with your refresh options. Additionally, you must have at least 8GB of free storage in the Windows 8.1 installation partitions i.e. 'C:'.

Remove everything and reinstall Windows

If you want to recycle your PC or start over completely, you can reset it to its factory settings.

Get started

Figure 313: Removing Everything and Reinstall Windows

# Advanced Startup

Advanced startup

Start up from a device or disc (such as a USB drive or DVD), change Windows startup settings, or restore Windows from a system image. This will restart your PC.

Restart now

Figure 314: Advanced Startup

Windows 8 and now Windows 8.1 have moved the advanced startup options within the Windows so, that they can only be access while needed and to speed up boot speed of Windows.

Advanced Startup option gives you the access to the following things:

1. Use startup behavior of Windows
2. Select whether to enable safe mode or not
3. Boot to Windows using external media
4. Recover Windows if window crash
5. Restore your PC from a system restore point or system recovery image.

**NOTE**

You will need a Windows installation media like a DVD or USB to avail this feature.

Your date, files, apps and personalization would be wiped from your PC.

Just press the 'Restart now' button and your Windows will restart and you would be able to select from advanced startup options of Windows.

261

**CHAPTER 15**

# Desktop & Modern-UI Integration

Windows 8.1 got the biggest interface changes in the history of Windows OS since Windows 8 where two different user interfaces were joined to work together in a single environment.

Microsoft also removed the well-known Start Button from taskbar of Windows 8 on desktop and instead, provided a new Start Screen thumbnail which appear when you mouse over on the left bottom corner. Now in windows 8.1, Microsoft has again added the Start button on taskbar which works, similarly, as that of Windows 7.

Windows 8 was left behind in major desktop and Modern-UI integration but, with the release of Windows 8.1, Microsoft has also improved the integration of Windows 8.1 Modern-UI and the desktop.

Microsoft has introduced many options and features in Windows 8.1 to make the desktop and Modern-UI integration richer.

The new features of the Windows 8.1 to help make the integration with Modern-UI more better are:

1. Start Button on taskbar to go to Start Screen
2. Option to boot directly to desktop
3. Option to go to 'All Apps' section
4. Option to view desktop apps first in 'All Apps' section
5. Use desktop wallpaper as Start Screen background

Let's have a closer look on each of the new features of Windows 8.1, described above.

# Boot to Desktop on Sign-in

1. Windows 8.1 has finally got the feature of booting directly to desktop instead of Start Screen but, this option isn't enabled by default.
2. You have to enable the option by going to taskbar properties.
3. Right click or tap and hold on taskbar. A pop up menu will appear. Here select 'Properties'.

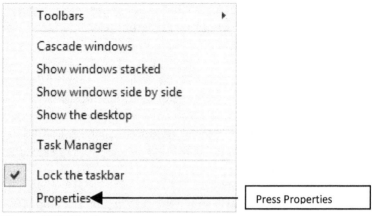

Figure 315: Toolbars

4. A pop up window will appear. Here press 'Navigation' button.

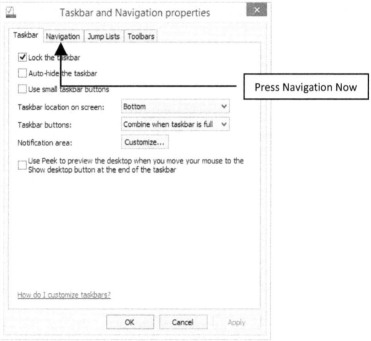

Figure 316: Taskbar and Navigations Properties

5. In the Navigation popup, Check 'Go to desktop instead of Start when I sign in'.

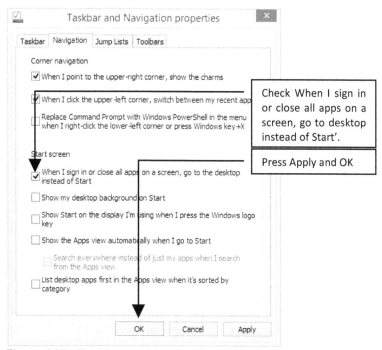

Figure 317: Taskbar and Navigation Properties

6. Press 'Apply' to save the settings.

Once saved, you would be taken directly to desktop instead of Start Screen when you sign-in for the next time.

# Start Button on Taskbar

Microsoft has finally decided to bring the Start Button from Windows 7 back in Windows 8.1 which was removed from Windows 8. The Start Button carries the Windows 8 logo and on pressing takes you to the Start Screen from desktop.

## NOTE

Now, in Windows 8.1, the Start Button can't be removed or disabled just like Windows 7.

# Same Background for Desktop and Modern-UI

Microsoft has decided to make the Windows 8.1 Modern-UI and desktop experience more common. It has introduced a new feature to make the desktop and Modern-UI experience more immersive and give them the same look by using the desktop wallpaper as Start Screen background.

You can enable the desktop wallpaper as Start Screen from two different locations:

➤ You can set up the desktop wallpaper as Start Screen background by going to Personalize options in Charms Bar.
➤ You can also use the desktop wallpaper as Start Screen background by enabling the option from Taskbar properties.

Now follow the instructions:

1. Simply go to the properties of taskbar by right clicking or tapping and holding on taskbar.

Figure 318:Taskbar

2.  Press Properties and the Properties pop up menu would open.

3.  Here navigate to the 'Navigation' tab by pressing it.

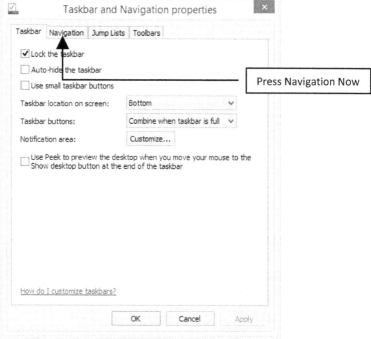

Figure 319: Taskbar and Navigation Properties

4.  Here check the 'Show my desktop background on Start'.

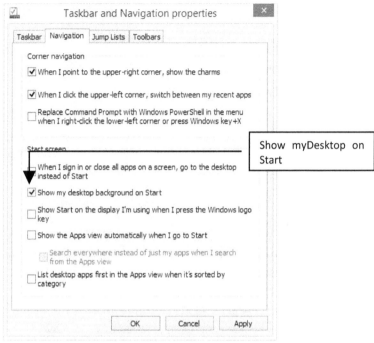

Figure 320: Taskbar and Navigation Properties

5. Press 'Apply' and you would have the desktop wallpaper as Start Screen background.

# All Apps View on Pressing the Start Button

If you are a desktop lover and don't want to use the tiled based Start Screen of Windows 8.1 then, you can always see the 'All Apps' view on Start where just the icons and the names of apps, installed on your PC, are showed instead of the tiles.

Microsoft has made it easy to view all apps instead of seeing the Start Screen.

Follow the Instructions:

1. Simply open taskbar Properties by right clicking or tapping and holding on taskbar.

2. Select Properties from small context menu.

Figure 321: Toolbars

3. A pop up window will open. Here navigate to 'Navigation' tab.

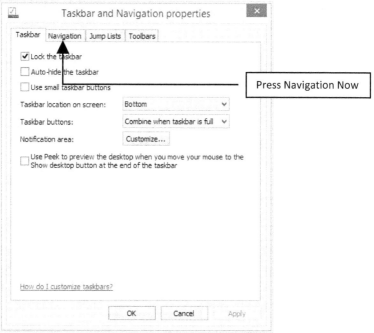

Figure 322: Taskbar and Navigation Properties

4. Check 'Show the Apps view automatically when I go to Start'.

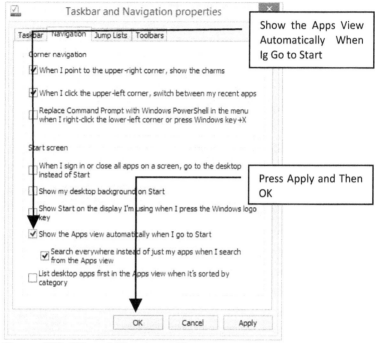

Figure 323: When I Sign In or Close

5.  Press 'Apply'. Next time you press the Start Button on taskbar or in Charms Bar, you would be taken to 'All Apps' view of Start Screen.

# Search from 'All Apps' Section

Windows 8.1 includes a rich and immersive search options, powered by Bing, which shows results from everywhere and everything at one place.

But, if you want to stick to the desktop and don't want to use the rich search experience, Microsoft has provided you the option to search just apps while using the 'Show All Apps view automatically when I go to Start' option which is enabled by default.

But, if you prefer to search using the rich experience and search everything, you may enable that easily.

1. Once you go to the taskbar 'Properties' by right clicking or tapping and holding on taskbar.
2. Here press 'Properties'.

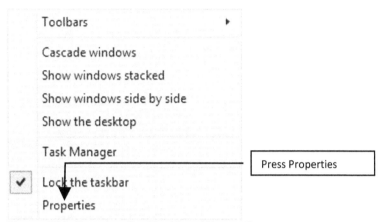

Figure 324: Opening the Taskbar / Properties

3. A pop up window will open.
4. Here Navigate to 'Navigation' tab.

Figure 325: Taskbar and Navigation Properties

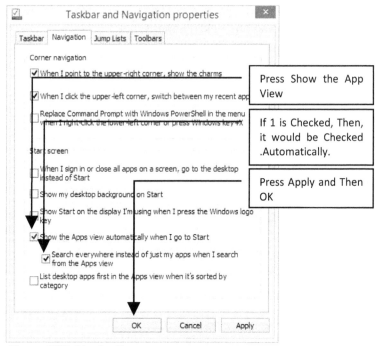

Figure 326: Navigation

5.  If you have checked the 'Show the Apps view automatically when I go to Start', then, you would see the 'Search everywhere instead of just my apps when I search from my apps view'. Check it.

6.  Press 'Apply' and you would be able to search everywhere for everything using the Search option.

# List of Desktop Apps First in Apps View

Windows 8.1 also lets you see the apps in 'All Apps' view sorted by desktop apps first so, that you don't have to search between desktop and Modern-UI apps.

If you are a desktop user and prefer not to use Modern-UI, this option is best for you. So, you don't get messed up between desktop and Modern-UI apps.

1. Simply go to 'Properties' of taskbar by right clicking or tapping and holding and pressing 'Properties'.

Figure 327: Taskbar

2. A pop-up window will open. Here navigate to 'Navigation' tab.

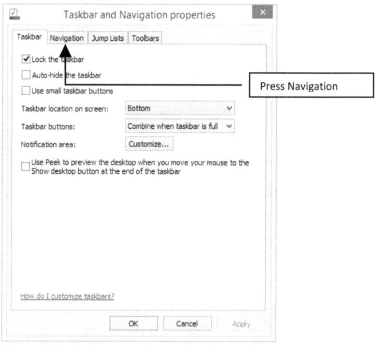

Figure 328: Taskbar and Navigation Properties

3. Check 'List desktop apps first in the Apps view when it's sorted by category'.

**NOTE**

You can't see the desktop apps first if you have sorted the apps by some other option like date of installed, name or by most used etc.

4. Press 'Apply' and the 'All Apps' section with category wise sorting will show desktop apps first.

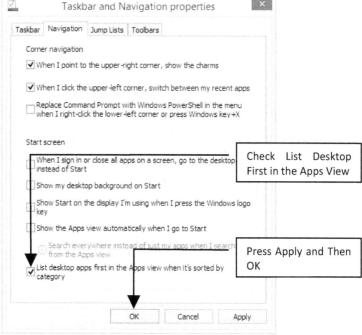

Figure 329: List Desktop App

**CHAPTER 16** »

# Snap

Windows has been well-known for its multi-tasking features and you could open and use multiple programs on the desktop.

But, with the release of Windows 8 and its new Modern-UI, Microsoft had to introduce a new multi-tasking feature for Modern-UI apps. Microsoft introduced a new feature of using two Modern-UI apps at a time which was named as Snap.

Although, Windows 8 solved the multi-tasking problems of Modern-UI and desktop apps with Snap mode where two different apps could be used at once on a screen but, the Snap in Windows 8 was limited.

You could only snap two apps at a time as there were two selective snap sizes only. The apps weren't configured to work in snap mode even the desktop couldn't be opened in small snap and Store app also wasn't compatible with snap.

Microsoft, with the release of Windows 8.1 has also improved the snap mode of Windows 8.1 and the most of the limitations have been removed from this awesome feature.

You can now snap multiple apps at a time, different sizes are available to be snapped and the almost all the apps now support small sizes. The best thing about the snap feature in Windows 8.1 is the ability to select where the apps would be snapped.

# How to Snap

If you want to snap different Modern-UI apps on your screen, simply select the app by pressing it from above or selecting it from recent apps list. Now, move it to different parts on screen.

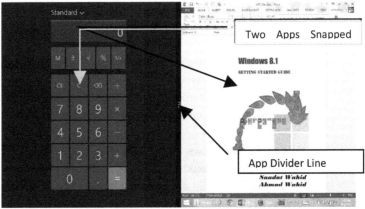

Figure 330: Two Apps Snapped

You will see a divider line on screen which shows that the app will be snapped. You can leave the app and the app will open up in snap.

# Resizing App Snaps

With Windows 8.1, you can now resize the app snaps and select different sizes for an app.

Simply move / drag the divider line between two snapped apps to resize the snap size.

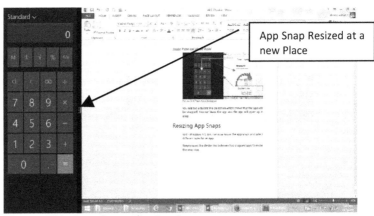

Figure 331: App Snap Resized

# Snap According to Resolution

The best and probably the biggest change in the snap mode of Windows 8.1 is the snap size dependency on screen resolutions. You would be able to snap more apps on a screen with big resolutions while screens with smaller resolutions would only allow two app snaps.

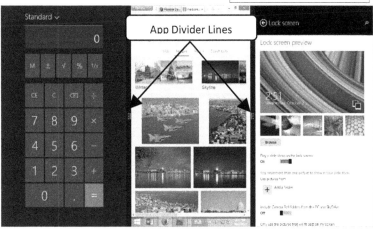

Figure 332: Three Apps Snapped

You can determine the snap possibilities on your screen by moving different apps in different snap positions.

Here are some common screen sizes and the number of apps which can be snapped:

1024 x 768   pixels = 2 snapped apps
1366 x 768   pixels = 2 snapped apps
1600 x 900   pixels = 3 snapped apps
1920 x 1080 pixels = 4 snapped apps

**NOTE**

The number of snap positions will keep increasing the screen resolutions.

**CHAPTER 17** >>>

# Keyboard Shortcuts for Use in Windows 8.1

# Keyboard Shortcuts  Functions

| | |
|---|---|
| *Alt+Esc* | Cycle through items in the order in which they were opened |
| *Alt+F4* | Close the active item, or exit the active app |
| *Alt+Page Down* | Move down one screen |
| *Alt+Page Up* | Move up one screen |
| *Alt+Spacebar* | Open the shortcut menu for the active window |
| *Alt+Tab* | Switch between open apps (except desktop apps) |
| *Alt+Underlined Letter* | Perform the command for that letter |
| *Ctrl+A* | Select all items in a document or window |
| *Ctrl+Alt+Tab* | Use the arrow keys to switch between all open apps |
| *Ctrl+C or Ctrl+Insert* | Copy the selected item |
| *Ctrl+D or (Delete)* | Delete the selected item and move it to the Recycle Bin |
| *Ctrl+Down Arrow* | Move the cursor to the beginning of the next paragraph |
| *Ctrl+Esc* | Open the Start screen |
| *Ctrl+F4* | Close the active document (in apps that allow you to have multiple documents open simultaneously) |
| *Ctrl+Left Arrow* | Move the cursor to the beginning of the previous word |
| *Ctrl+Mouse Scroll Wheel* | Change the size of desktop icons or zoom in or out of a large number of items, like apps pinned to the Start screen |
| *Ctrl+Right Arrow* | Move the cursor to the beginning of the next word |
| *Ctrl+Scroll Wheel* | Zoom in or out of a large number of items, like apps pinned to the Start screen |
| *Ctrl+Shift + Esc* | Open Task Manager |
| *Ctrl+Shift with an Arrow Key* | Select a block of text |
| *Ctrl+Up Arrow* | Move the cursor to the beginning of the previous paragraph |
| *Ctrl+V or Shift+Insert* | Paste the selected item |
| *Ctrl+X* | Cut the selected item |
| *Ctrl+Y* | Redo an action |
| *Ctrl+ Z* | Undo an action |
| *Esc* | Stop or exit the current task |

| | |
|---|---|
| *Esc* | Stop or leave the current task |
| *F1* | Display Help |
| *F10* | Activate the menu bar in the active app |
| *F2* | Rename the selected item |
| *F3* | Search for a file or folder |
| *F4* | Display the address bar list in File Explorer |
| *F5* | Refresh the active window |
| *F6* | Cycle through screen elements in a window or on the desktop |
| *Shift+Delete* | Delete the selected item without moving it to the Recycle Bin first |
| *Shift+F10* | Display the shortcut menu for the selected item |
| *WIN Key* | Display or hide the Start screen |
| *WIN Key+,* | Temporarily peek at the desktop |
| *WIN Key+Alt+Number* | Open the Jump List for the desktop app pinned to the taskbar in the position indicated by the number |
| *WIN Key+B* | Set focus in the notification area |
| *WIN Key+C* | Open the Charms |
| *WIN Key+C* | Open the charms |
| | In an app, open the commands for the app |
| *WIN Key+Ctrl+B* | Switch to the app that displayed a message in the notification area |
| *WIN Key+Ctrl+F* | Search for PCs (if you're on a network) |
| *WIN Key+Ctrl+Number* | Switch to the last active window of the desktop app pinned to the taskbar in the position indicated by the number |
| *WIN Key+Ctrl+ Shift+Number* | Open a new instance of the desktop app located at the given position on the taskbar as an administrator |
| *WIN Key+Ctrl+Tab* | Cycle through open apps (except desktop apps) and snaps them as they are cycled |
| *WIN Key+Ctrl+Tab* | Cycle through open apps (except desktop apps) and snap them as they are cycled |
| *WIN Key+D* | Display and hide the desktop |
| *WIN Key+Down Arrow* | Minimize the desktop window |
| *WIN Key+E* | Open Computer |
| *WIN Key+Enter* | Open Narrator |
| *WIN Key+F* | Open the Search charm to search files |
| *WIN Key+F* | Open the Search charm and search for files |
| *WIN Key+F1* | Open Windows Help and Support |
| *WIN Key+H* | Open the Share charm |
| *WIN Key+H* | Open the Share charm |
| *WIN Key+I* | Open the Settings charm |

| | |
|---|---|
| *WIN Key+I* | Open the Settings charm |
| *WIN Key+K* | Open the Devices charm |
| *WIN Key+L* | Lock your PC or switch users |
| *WIN Key+Left Arrow* | Maximize the desktop window to the left side of the screen |
| *WIN Key+M* | Minimize all windows |
| *WIN Key+Number* | Start the desktop app pinned to the taskbar in the position indicated by the number. If the app is already running, switch to that app. |
| *WIN Key+O* | Lock device orientation |
| *WIN Key+P* | Choose a presentation display mode |
| *WIN Key+Page Up* | Move the Start screen and apps to the monitor on the left (apps in the desktop won't change monitors) |
| *WIN Key+Pause* | Display the System Properties dialog box |
| *WIN Key+Pg Down* | Move the Start screen and apps to the monitor on the right (Apps in the desktop won't change monitors) |
| *WIN Key+Pg Up* | Move the Start screen and apps to the monitor on the left (Apps in the desktop won't change monitors) |
| *WIN Key+Plus (+) or Minus (-)* | Zoom in or out using Magnifier |
| *WIN Key+Q* | Open the Search charm to search apps |
| *WIN Key+Q* | Open the Search charm and search for apps |
| *WIN Key+R* | Open the Run dialog box |
| *WIN Key+Right Arrow* | Maximize the desktop window to the right side of the screen |
| *WIN Key+Shift+Number* | |
| *WIN Key+Shift+Tab* | Cycle through open apps (except desktop apps) in reverse order |
| *WIN Key+Shift+Tab* | Cycle through open apps (except desktop apps) in reverse order |
| *WIN Key+Start Typing* | Search your PC |
| *WIN Key+T* | Cycle through apps on the taskbar |
| *WIN Key+Tab* | Cycle through open apps (except desktop apps) |
| *WIN Key+Tab* | Cycle through open apps (except desktop apps) |
| *WIN Key+U* | Open Ease of Access Center |
| *WIN Key+Up Arrow* | Maximize the desktop window |
| *WIN Key+W* | Open the Search charm to search settings |

| | |
|---|---|
| *WIN Key+W* | Open the Search charm and search for settings |
| *WIN Key+X* | Open the Quick Link menu |
| *WIN Key+Esc* | Exit Magnifier |
| *WIN Key+K* | Open the Devices charm |
| *WIN Key+Page Down* | Move the Start screen and apps to the monitor on the right (apps in the desktop won't change monitors) |

# Detailed Table of Content

| Chapter | Topic | Pg, No. |
|---------|-------|---------|

# About the Authors

*Saadat Wahid, Muzzammil Waheed and Ahmad Wahid*

# Saadat Wahid

Saadat Wahid, the primary author, has a HDR in Finance, two master degrees, a long list of training & development programs in IT and Management (both attended and conducted) and a 25+ years of corporate related exposure at his credentials.

Apart from his attachment with many research and academic organizations, he has deep interest in the computer and information technology. Long working / classroom training / OJT of Windows since the era of Windows 3.1, facilitation of many software development programs and maintenance of many technology blogs encouraged the author to go ahead with the book on Windows 8.1.

The success of his previous book; 'Understanding Windows 8.1', has also encouraged the author to move toward training-oriented and applied approach to the Getting Started Guide for the Windows 8.1. He has applied the illustrated approach of training while developing the current book; Windows 8.1, by adding graphical display to each and every function, included in the new version of Windows 8.1 by Microsoft.

His other publications are; 'An Applied Analysis of Financial Performance of Commercial Banks', 'Faculty & Stress', 'Understanding Windows 8.1' and 'A Contemporary Study on Stock Behavior of Financial Institutions'.

His current engagements are in many institutions of higher learning as faculty & Researcher, corporate consultancy, development activities and freelance writing.

## Contacts

| | |
|---|---|
| Email: | saadat_wahid@yahoo.com |
| | saadat@knowledge_news.com |
| Facebook | https://www.facebook.com/SaadatWahid |
| Google+ | http://bit.ly/SaadatWahidGPlus |

# Muzzammil Waheed

13+ years of professional experience in designing and developing enterprise solutions like Auto and Equipment Industry data processing, Healthcare Staffing management, Data integration platforms, Ecommerce Platforms, Web2Print and MIS solutions for Print Industry, Logistics management, ecommerce B2B and B2c portals, Web Search engines, Inventory and order management systems, Document management systems, Banking and leasing systems, Content management systems, CRM solutions, Mathematical optimization for solving complex problems.

Directing multiple projects from management and architectural design point of view.

Specialties: Managing multiple projects, User interface Design, User Experience, Architechture Design, Solution Design of business problems and scenarios, Cutting Edge Technology, Sharepoint Customization, SharePoint Development, SaaS, SOA, Distributed and scalable systems, .NET Framework and technologies including silverlight 4.0, WPF, WCF, WF, Web 2.0 & Ajax based applications.

Other than the above services, he also operates his own online printing service i.e. myprintcloud.com and he is also the founder of Windows8Core.com.

**Contact**

**Email**   muzamilw@hotmail.com
my.linkedin.com/pub/muzzammil-waheed/8/86b/6b6/

# *Ahmad Wahid*

This teen-aged University sophomore in commerce is, currently, writing on many tech blogs. He started writing on his own blogs in mid-2011 while he was in junior college.

Immediately after the launch of Windows 8 Developer Preview in September 2011, he launched a specific blog on the Windows 8 as Co-Founder and Editor In-Chief, in collaboration with an IT specialist. This Windows 8 blog moved to same heights like the Windows 8. Now, in a short span of one and a half years, this blog has been ranked as 3 with wide global acknowledgement and repute. This blog is known not only as the source of latest information on Windows 8 and 8.1 but also as a major contributor toward the tips and tricks.

## Contacts

| | |
|---|---|
| Email: | ahmadwahid@outlook.com, |
| | ahmad@windows8core.com |
| Facebook | https://www.fb.com/m.ahmad.wahid |
| Twitter | twitter.com/ahmadwahid1 |

www.ingramcontent.com/pod-product-compliance
Lightning Source LLC
Chambersburg PA
CBHW071407050326
40689CB00010B/1787